BUILDING FOR
MODERN MAN

BUILDING FOR

MODERN MAN

A SYMPOSIUM

EDITED BY THOMAS H. CREIGHTON

ESSAY INDEX

Essay Index Reprint Series

106697

 BOOKS FOR LIBRARIES PRESS
FREEPORT, NEW YORK

STANDARD BOOK NUMBER:

8369-1029-X

LIBRARY OF CONGRESS CATALOG CARD NUMBER:

74-80385

PRINTED IN THE UNITED STATES OF AMERICA

PREFACE

I̵N THE spring of 1947 some sixty persons whose lives are devoted to the study of man's physical environment were invited to Princeton University to engage in a two-day Conference. The official occasion was Conference Five of Series Two of the academic conferences that marked Princeton's Bicentennial Celebration. The result was a gathering of architects and planners, those who teach architecture and planning, those who write about such subjects, and a sprinkling of those who are engaged in related design fields. Twenty-four prepared papers were read, and in the eight sessions of the Conference a number of extemporaneous rebuttals, refutations, concurrences, and variations were added to the discussion.

As might be imagined, the topics under consideration spilled over the time limits of the formal session meetings and were further pursued in small group discussions at breakfast, lunch, and dinner, and far into the several nights that the participants spent together at the Princeton Inn. To some those postscript gatherings were more inspiring than the formal sessions. Apprised that this book was under preparation, one participant wrote the editor, "The gain at the Conference was the same that a political convention has. It is the electricity in the air . . . How in the hell can you get *that* into a book?"

The answer, of course, is that you can't. And yet the attempt to capture in print some of the areas of agreement and disagreement that were indicated at the Conference—some of the hope and resolve, and some of the frustration and discouragement—seemed to a number of the people who were there to be worth while. The attempt seemed to have purpose, in fact, to all but four of the participants. One, for the reasons stated above, felt that the effort would be useless. Two others stated quite flatly that they felt nothing worth saying had been said at the Conference, modestly including their own remarks with the others. A fourth believes that only he added anything of import to man's knowledge during the discussions, and since his words apparently fell on deaf ears he has lost interest in the matter. All of the other people who took part in or listened to the sessions have endorsed this permanent record, although not all of them have added papers. Some are frankly inarticulate (not all designers and planners express themselves well in words) and some feel that better men than they have said very nearly what they would say.

This book is not intended to be a factual *report* of the Princeton Conference. That meeting is the basis from which the discussion springs, but a serious and, I hope, fairly successful attempt has been made to draw into it some of the things that were said, or perhaps merely thought, by participants who were prevented by time, bashfulness, or the limitations of a fairly rigid agenda from getting themselves on the official record. Practically all of the original statements have been rewritten—some lengthened, some shortened, some radically revised. Very nearly half of the papers that follow were written after the Conference.

Before the gathering at Princeton the committee—in particular its indefatigable chairman, Arthur Holden— carried on a fairly extensive correspondence with those who had been invited. The Conference topics were discussed by letter, and "points of view" were established by a number of the participants. Pre-Conference discussions were held in New York and Boston and they resulted in further correspondence. All of these letters were made available while the book was being edited, and the introductions to each of the sections that follow are used as an opportunity to quote from them.

While the relation of this symposium to the Conference from which it sprang is being discussed, it should be pointed out that the program followed at Princeton is, with certain changes, the framework of the book.

The sequence of topics follows a logical pattern. The first three sections have to do with "analytical inquiry," the fourth is an interlude devoted to the subject of education, the fifth and sixth are concerned with "application of principles." The seventh is a personal debate with, perhaps, wider implications. The eighth and final section is a summary and a drawing of conclusions.

Within that framework the relation and order of subjects is equally obvious. Beginning with an inquiry into the environmental needs of man, as an individual and as a member of society, the discussion moves to a consideration of the various limitations (and conversely the possibilities) which physical, technical, and economic factors impose on the designer and the people for whom he designs. Thence the route is through a study of form—philosophical bases, physiological reception, and psychological effect—to an inquiry into how these matters should be taught.

With the next two sections the symposium moves to a more direct discussion of methods of application of the principles of design, on two planes—the planning of the more extensive environment, and the planning of buildings.

It would be very easy to overestimate the importance of this discussion, either because of the wide range of subject matter (which is perhaps too great for careful examination of each topic) or because of the galaxy of "great" names (not all of whom are as competent in words as they are in architecture or planning). However, it would be incorrect to consider the collection of papers presented here as simply another symposium, of which there have been many in recent years. This is a direct statement, the synthesis of many varying attitudes, by the designing professions in evaluation of their own work, at the end of one era and the beginning of another.

We are, for better or worse, finally leaving the period of eclecticism and entering on a serious search for an idiom appropriate to our time. If any one point can mark that change, it seems to be this fifth decade of the twentieth century. Advanced souls have called for it long since—before Sullivan; perhaps before Greenough—and some of the very people represented in this discussion have been saying for many years nearly the same things they put in fresh words here. On the other hand, the practice of eclecticism will undoubtedly continue to produce much of the man-made environment for many years to come. There is not, and there will not be, a sharp dividing line between two "periods" of design. Rather, the new era has crept up on us without any full evaluation of its implications. There is a greater understanding of man's importance and a greater desire to understand the society he moves in—even, in many parts of the world, a desire to change the form of that society. There is a gradually awakening realization of the possibilities for radically improving our environment, and a sober acceptance of the limitations which the new techniques imply. There has been a gradual understanding that a new philosophy of form is required if planning and architecture are to keep pace with the other sciences and arts and disciplines.

Here, then, is a statement of principles for our time, and a discussion of ways to apply those principles. To some it may seem confused, inconsistent, inconclusive. Was there ever anything but confusion at the end of an epoch or inconsistency at the beginning? Is there clear-cut decision on the political front, or the educational, or even the scientific? If there were consistency or complete agreement, it would be something to worry about; there are already too many small cliques in architecture as in other fields that are sure of their direction and contemptuous of any other. Conclusiveness will come after the fact, not before. Conclusion is a historian's prerogative—exploration the designer's, and evaluation the critic's.

For other reasons also the papers seem important to many of the participants. One thing that is significant is that although the discussion is on an academic level, it deals in the most important sense with actualities. When Konrad Wachsmann speaks of the possibilities and limitations of industrialized machine processes, he is thinking of his prefabricated house which is going into production at the moment. Henry Churchill and Louis Justement took time off from actual community plan studies to express their thoughts on community planning. Ernest Kump had just finished a study of the nature of an actual community in order to determine what sort of school it needed when he delivered his dictum that "when we know man, then we can plan." Walter Baermann draws his conclusions about the influence of merchandising from daily contact with merchandisers. The list could go on and include the greater part of the gathering.

So the positions in the papers that follow, "advanced" as they may seem to some readers, are no longer theoretical. Many theoreticians and teachers are represented, but the prime significance of this symposium and the time in which it is published is that it deals with matters which have become pressing practical problems. As John Burchard says, "The great figures, many of whom are here, did the stable-cleaning. They reaffirmed the axioms." At this time, then, it is right to consider the axioms accepted and explore specific principles and their application.

It is significant, too, that the writers, the historians, the teachers, and the critics who are represented have an opportunity to discuss with, lecture to, criticize, and measure the practitioners who took part in the proceedings. Sigfried Giedion in his way and Talbot Hamlin in his and Joseph Hudnut in another manner make their appeals for an emotional quality in architectural form to a group which could, by its design and the influence of its design, carry the impulse into important actuality. That fact seems to color the way things are said, and to give them greater import than they would otherwise have. Adelbert Ames's philosophy of esthetics is not an academic presentation—facing architects, he translated its implications into architectural terms. There is in the discussion a meeting of the theoretical and the practical; the subjective and the objective.

There is very nearly unanimous agreement that the axioms *have* been established. They are fairly well defined by the topics discussed: that there is a humanistic basis for all planning; that the new technical possibilities carry certain limitations with them; that the new esthetic is based on physiological and psychological grounds. There is agreement about these attitudes, and the discussion is of ways and means to apply them. (For example, the question of the psychological need for an emotional content above pure mechanism; the question of whether there is danger of worship of the machine instead of use of the machine.) This is true despite the fact that many points of view are represented. True, only one voice was raised in open defense of eclecticism, and the reader will not find it since it was eliminated at the request of the author. A decade earlier the meeting would have been the usual sad battle between "modernists" and "traditionalists." The divergence in this assemblage of personalities is not along those lines—all are agreed on the basic architectural traditions, and the differences lie in methods of specific application. For instance, there is a group of CIAM adherents. And there is Roger Greeley. And Ralph Walker, and Arthur Holden, and Robert O'Connor. Then there is William Wurster, whose work has recently been given a new style label by the critics who strain to catalog. There are Roland Wank and Henry Kamphoefner and Gordon Lorimer, whose work represents many different attitudes and springs from many disparate urges. Yet here, in the discussion that follows, they talk together and find areas of agreement—perhaps more clearly an agreement than a definition of their disagreements.

There are many great names represented—Frank Lloyd Wright and Walter Gropius and Richard Neutra among others—and one criticism of the discussion might be that they state their positions rather dogmatically, and in some cases use the privilege of the accepted great to close their ears to other points of view. This, however, is rare; there is a remarkable interplay of opinions.

Finally, the group is an unusual one in that it represents many fields of design and related disciplines. There are the architects and their professorial colleagues, but there are also the planners of the larger environment (practitioners and teachers), designers of the more limited individual objects, and the engineers. In addition to that, there are several philosophers and psychologists who have been led in their studies to a consideration of the effect on man of man's designed environment.

Surely there is an opportunity here for a group statement (or a series of individual statements from which the reader can draw his own conclusions), which should be important. Whether it is important is for someone more objective than the editor to decide. I have worked over these papers too long to know any more whether they may seem as vital to others as they seem to me. In any event, they stand here for guidance, for reference, and for possible study. It will be possible for students of later generations to say that this is what *we* were. It is as complete a statement of the position of architecture in the middle of the twentieth century as the practicing and criticizing profession can make for itself. From this point we go on.

T.H.C.

CONTENTS

CONTENTS

CONTENTS

THE SOCIAL BASIS
OF DESIGN

INTRODUCTION

BY THOMAS H. CREIGHTON

ARCHITECTURE begins with the study of man. This seems like an obvious statement, but a full discussion of its implications had been missing from too many symposia and conferences of an academic nature before the Princeton meeting. Man and the society within which he moves are always theoretically the concern of the designer; yet through long periods of design and building this responsibility has been forgotten, brushed aside, or paid mere lip service. What the participants here are discussing is the planning of *man's* physical environment—the modification of natural environment by planning and building structures and communities in a way best suited to *man* of our time.

The subject matter seems obvious, but the implications which arise are far from obvious ones. Pre-Conference correspondence among the participants indicated an interest in two aspects of the question—the need to study man *of our time*, with all his particular social, personal, and political requirements; and, even more fundamentally, the need to affirm strongly the inevitable *historic* social basis of architecture. Walter Gropius felt that the rediscovery of this fundamental fact should be stressed. He wrote:

> The social problem should come first because everything is related to it, and this is perhaps the most important rediscovery of our contemporary period. Whether an architect does a small building or a whole community in design, without understanding the basic elements of the social life involved he will not be able to make his contribution fit the whole.

George Howe questioned whether any group of architects previous to our time had studied man's total social needs. He replied to Dr. Gropius:

> I don't see why you speak of the social problem as a *re-discovery*. As far as my knowledge goes it was never be-

fore the prime mover in building design. The substitution of the religion of social man for the religions of man-gods and god-man is interesting and instructive to consider.

But Dr. Gropius, feeling that the architect's concern with man and his society had simply been lost for a time, insisted on the correctness of the word *rediscovery*. He responded:

I was trying to compare the oneness of life and form-expression during great creative periods of the past with the incoherent bits of chaotic design during the "art for art's sake" period which we have just passed through. It might be that the designer of the great periods has only been subconsciously aware of the social relationships in his work and that it was left to our generation to seek a conscious intellectual approach.

Other participants made a point of the need to understand the particular characteristics of our society, as distinguished from previous ones. In a letter expressing the point of view which is developed in his paper that follows, Arthur E. Morgan wrote:

It seems to me that architecture and the related arts tend strongly to reflect philosophies of life and of society. For instance, we could scarcely think of a democratic country building the Egyptian pyramids. When people have newly won their freedom, however, they imitate those they formerly envied. Architecture has suffered from that disability. It tends to continue the traditions of a feudal society. Until recently nearly all public buildings continued the traditions of a social order we had theoretically repudiated. The elements of competitive ostentation and conspicuous waste in American architecture have been much reduced in recent years, but not eliminated.

Henry Churchill echoed this point of view, while urging the Conference to "give some thought to the relationship, *today*, of the architect to his world." He agreed that "architecture is an architect's expression of his time and place," while pointing out the "place means not just geographical location, but social status." Note how very different this concept is from the usual one that architecture is *the expression* of a given social period. Churchill's point is that it reflects the *architect's* place in society. He expanded this idea in a pre-Conference letter as follows:

It must be remembered that the term *conspicuous waste* is not necessarily one of reproach nor does it necessarily imply something meretricious. It is an explanation of a state of mind, which has a characteristic physical expression. . . . There are two kinds of architecture: shelter and honorific. The first has two subdivisions: the simply useful, and that which has an added element of conspicuous waste in greater or less degree. The second has two subdivisions: the simply useless, and that which tries to combine the honorific and the useful. This latter sometimes is identical with and sometimes is merely confused with the second subdivision of shelter architecture.*

The shelter architecture of the little man has been impermanent and has vanished. Only the great and the rich, the rulers of the ancient corporate states, could build permanently. The architect worked for them or not at all—he was no free agent. In Egypt he built temples for the priests, in Rome he constructed mighty works for the State, in the Middle Ages edifices for God and the princes of the Church, and in the Renaissance palaces for successful gangsters. The eighteenth century and the Industrial Revolution both profoundly affected relationships between the architect and his work. The eighteenth century made the architect think of his work not as an expression of society but as an expression of himself. The Industrial Revolution, by removing the preparation of structural material from the site to the factory, turned the Master Builder into a Chief Draftsman, removed the architect from contact with and sense

* Compare this point of view, and Dr. Morgan's, with that expressed in Ralph Walker's paper in Section III. Walker distinguishes between "proletarian" and "aristocratic" architecture.—Ed.

of the physical materials of building. He became a paper eclectic, out of touch with reality.

The importance of historical study in reaching a full understanding of the social basis of design is not carried further in the papers that follow, principally because all of the discussants seemed agreed that the architect's relation to society *today* and *today's* social requirements from architecture are the matters which need emphasis. Henry Kamphoefner demurred:

It seems to me that the fundamentals of good architecture have been developing since the beginnings of recorded history . . . a full understanding of the accomplishments of architecture through recorded history is vital for a thorough understanding of contemporary architecture, its animus, and its destiny.

While no one disagreed with that statement, there was a general feeling that now is the time to look for our own problems and their own solutions. Joseph Hudnut wrote:

We cannot understand the present without an experience of history, but could we not take it for granted that everyone present has had such an experience? . . . history can be made to prove almost anything; in fact, that seems to be its principal purpose in the scheme of things.

While the statements that follow say nothing revolutionary, they add up to a challenge to the architects of today to study man and his present social needs, to develop a program from those requirements, and to find ways to activate that program. The only disagreement is one of emphasis: Should we put most stress on the study, which has been so long neglected, or should we now pay more attention to the action in planning, which has been so long in coming—or can the two activities be carried on simultaneously? Ernest Kump's reiterated insistence that "when we know man, then we can plan," clashes somewhat with assumptions on the part of others that we do now know a great deal about man and his present needs. Carlos Contreras advocates a plan to live more simply and more slowly. William Roger Greeley believes we must separate the large city into neighborhoods, and strengthen the small town—a common plea that is not challenged until Theodore McCrosky's paper in Section v. At one point during the Conference Henry Churchill, expressing the concern of a number of participants that the architect's interest in social matters might become almost patronizing, remarked, "There seems to be a tendency to tell man what he needs, instead of trying to find out."

The human and social basis of design, as a subject, could not be confined to the discussion in this first Section. It spills over into the papers which deal with the matter of democratic planning in Section v, it colors the interpretation of the visual sensations in Section iii, it influences the points made about technological advance in Section ii. Each part of the Conference was influenced by studies of man and society that are being made.

The fact that this subject of "the abiding humanistic values of architecture," as one observer expressed it, permeates all of the Conference papers may mark the importance of this gathering. Whether or not there is agreement on solutions or even emphasis, the unanimity of insistence that architecture and planning begin with man in society certainly signifies the end of the "paper eclectic" as the pretender to the planner's role, and the acceptance, as Dr. Gropius would have it, of a "conscious intellectual approach" to architecture as a social science.

NEW USES: NEW FORMS

BY ARTHUR C. HOLDEN

Arthur Holden, architect (Fellow of the American Institute of Architects), author, lecturer, student of the social and economic phases of architecture, planning, and housing, was Chairman of the Princeton Conference. His indefatigable work before and during the discussions impressed all of the participants, and it is appropriate that the first statement (as well as the final one) should be his. His paper presents simply the premise that changing social conditions bring changing uses for buildings and, in time, new forms which affect our environment.

THERE is significance in any change of emphasis, but there is especial significance in the increasing recognition that man has lost control of the shaping of his physical environment. As man's intellectual progress has enabled him to utilize mechanical means vastly to increase his physical power, why, at such a time, has man's physical environment grown less satisfactory? To reverse the tendency it is necessary to analyze and attempt to control forces which appear to have been blindly shaping man's physical surroundings along lines that are not desirable.

As we look back, the past two hundred years have been years of phenomenal change. Man has changed the methods of supplying his needs from one of individual production and almost individual self-sufficiency to the method which has made man part of an organization and has so mechanized his processes of production that he can do little effective work as an individual unless he can utilize tools and machinery which have been prepared for him by others. These new tools are not only far more complex than traditional handicraft tools but they are interrelated with a complex system of power production and power distribution. A basic part of the complexities of the system has been the contractual obligations which have grown up as a result of every man's dependence upon the work of others.

Man has had visual evidence that fundamental changes were taking place. He has seen steamship transportation by rail and water replace the stagecoach and the sailing ship. As the power-operated factory, with its intricate machinery, has replaced the processes of the handicrafts, he has observed the differences in both the quantity and the quality of the articles produced. Our own generation has seen the automobile replace the horse and necessitate a complete rebuilding of our highway system. Now we are witnessing the navigation of the air by planes moving more rapidly than we had believed it possible for man-made engines to navigate.

ARTHUR C. HOLDEN

The visual evidence of these changes in method is before
us, but what is less evident is the significance of the change
in scale, and the changes in human relationships, which
our new equipment has brought about. Perhaps the change
in scale has been the most remarkable of all. To accomplish
the material results which we see about us, men have had
to live and work in new ways. Modern methods of living
and working require large numbers of people to come together for many different purposes.

We must recognize that it is a natural human tendency
to meet a new demand by seizing upon something that
already exists and adapting it to a new use. When demands
are made for larger buildings for new uses, the first resort
is to take some existing form and adapt it quickly to the
use desired. Gradually the form is altered and a new type
evolves. Still later comes the realization that the new form
and new use have a far-reaching effect upon environment.

As we look back over history, we realize that the types
of buildings which provided for large assemblies of people
were relatively limited. In ancient times both markets and
pageants were held out of doors in public squares. Ancient
religious ceremonies were performed in impressive temples. These were later dwarfed by the great cathedrals of
the Christian era. Both the Romans and the Greeks built
large theatres and open amphitheatres to accommodate the
spectators of the drama and athletic games. The largest
spaces put under roof by the Romans were their great public baths, which were important meeting places and centers of social life.

In all periods of history, emperors and princes were able
to command great residential buildings. Palace architecture has always offered an example of large-scale building.
It is perhaps significant that when Americans were first
confronted with large-scale structural problems they
naively found themselves describing their products as "palace" river steamers and "palace" hotels, or even "palace"
theatres.

In New York City there are some interesting examples

of the part scale plays in the evolution of new forms and the use of a recognized precedent through adaptation. When the Pennsylvania Railroad was projecting extending its tracks into Manhattan, it presented the problem of planning a station comprising the largest area that had ever been enclosed under one roof as a single piece of construction. The architects looked to the great Roman baths for a precedent. The parallel was a good one so far as space distribution and roofing problems were concerned, even though the uses accommodated were almost completely dissimilar. Both the Pennsylvania Station and the Grand Central, which followed it shortly, represent important steps in the history of design. Yet even though the architects of the Grand Central used new forms for the interior of the great concourse, they resorted to an inflated copy of the little Musée Galliére for the 42nd Street façade.

The historical importance of these two structures stems from the fact that they were linked with the past, on the one hand; while, on the other, they represented a link with the future. In both buildings, advances were made in the segregation of vehicular and pedestrian approaches. The design of the Grand Central included a pioneering attempt to isolate on an upper level all vehicular traffic which needed to by-pass the station. Here stands out a recognition, even though expressed in timid terms, that scale in use as well as scale in the size of the structure creates new problems to be solved in the relation of the design of the building to the design of its environment.

Thus it seems clear that any attempt to improve man's physical environment must begin with a study of today's human relationships, the new environmental problems they raise and the new concepts in scale they imply. It might be stated as a premise from which to start the discussion that these new human and social requirements cannot be met by an unthinking or a stubborn adherence to past forms, but rather by a full understanding of how those forms in past ages satisfied the requirements for proper physical environment in their times.

CARLOS CONTRERAS

SIMPLICITY LEADS TO
GOOD DESIGN

BY CARLOS CONTRERAS

Born in Mexico in 1892, Mr. Contreras has become known as one of that country's outstanding architects. His contact with cultural development in the United States has been intimate, however, as he was educated at Columbia University where he taught French, Spanish, and Design and Elements of Architecture, between 1918 and 1925. In addition to teaching at the National Preparatory School and at the National University of Mexico and practicing architecture, he has been (1929 to 1948) a representative of the John Simon Guggenheim Memorial Foundation, a four-time delegate to the International Congress of City Planning, and an active or honorary member of many professional societies here and abroad.

Mr. Contreras writes with deep feeling of the need for simplicity in our lives and in our architecture. At the Princeton Conference he spoke extemporaneously of an experience in elementary community planning and building in a small village in Mexico in a manner to move all of the participants deeply. That exposition, which depended on spontaneity and personal contact with the speaker for its effectiveness, gave one a concrete realization of what is meant by the *human* basis of architecture. Contreras' life in Mexico and the United States makes him sure of his thesis that human requirements are met best in a simple life, and that simplicity leads to good design.

I THINK we should see what factors influence man's physical environment and what factors influence design and composition; from the study of these elements we may find the right course to follow in defining the human and the social basis of design.

First there are the *people*, the human groups of men, women, and children. Their races, ages, occupations; their creeds, their customs; the way they dress, how they play, what they eat; how and where they now live—these factors affect life, and they affect design.

Then there is the *size* of these human groups: their number and quality are also factors that influence design. As

· 11 ·

the size of the human groups increases, the problems of life and organization become more complex. Social *units* of different types are born. Social *needs* of various kinds appear. The economic status of the individual and of the community becomes more and more important. Some become rich—the more remain poor. In the past these phenomena of the growth of human groups just happened—in most cases, haphazardly—and so we are almost always faced with the problem of correcting evils and correcting the living conditions of these human groups.

Thus the *social authority of government* must be provided with the necessary financial elements to furnish the human groups with all their social needs: water, sewage disposal, streets, gardens, schools, hospitals, homes.

There are other factors that affect design, of course. The site is an essential influence: a flat meadow, a mountain ridge, a lake, or a river front, the sea. The climate is another element of influence: the land with snow-capped mountains, the temperate zones, the tropics, the dominating winds, the amount of rain or snow, the sun.

The natural materials that the human groups have at hand to build with have a bearing upon design. But we are concerned here with the human and social basis of design.

In the past man's environmental needs were met and satisfied very simply because his life was simple and his needs were few. He was sturdier and he lived more slowly. His day and his night were longer than ours. Biologically he lived better. He seldom improved on nature because the beauty of nature as he found it and as he saw it satisfied him. Now—almost always—we try to improve upon nature, and we are not always successful.

Man's environmental needs in the future will be better satisfied if we combine respect for and attachment to nature with the application of design. In that way our environment will not be forced upon us: it will grow with us, be a part of ourselves, giving us a sense of tranquillity, a feeling of peace and well-being, a true enjoyment of life.

Man's needs for shelter have changed, but our tendency

in designing man's home must be to simplify instead of to complicate our lives within that home. The simpler our lives, the simpler our homes should be and the better we shall live in them. Man's esthetic, intellectual, emotional, and spiritual needs must be strengthened. More attention must be given to these human needs. To satisfy them with adequate design, in small or large human groups, will mean the satisfaction of human and social needs of importance. The social needs of all human groups must tend toward simplicity—and *simplicity leads to good design.*

The excessive growth of population in our cities; the excessive speed at which we live; the killing pace of our urban life; the unbalanced and unjust difference of economic levels; the social injustice of poverty and scarcity; the shameful living conditions—throughout the world—in all slums of all kinds; these things affect and influence the living individual and social habits of mankind, and therefore affect and influence design. At the same time these social evils can and must be corrected to a great extent through the simplicity and quality of good design: human design—social design—architectural design—planning design.

Let us then *plan* to live more simply, to live more slowly. Let us give of what we have to satisfy the needs of others and let us, above all, live in harmony with our neighbors and specially, very specially, with ourselves.

SOCIAL AND VISUAL UNITS

BY WILLIAM ROGER GREELEY

Carlos Contreras' appeal for simplicity in living and simplicity in design—the appeal of a man who has spent time helping simple people in simple villages in Mexico plan a better environment for themselves—is followed by a similar call for simple living in small units, with as little modification of nature's environment as possible, from an architect who practices in a large urban center in the United States.

William Roger Greeley was born in Lexington, Massachusetts, in 1881. Educated at the Massachusetts Institute of Technology, he has worked and practiced since in that same state. A member of the firm of Kilham, Hopkins and Greeley, Architects, he is a Fellow of the American Institute of Architects and a member of the Regional Planning Association of America.

PROFOUND dissatisfaction with present social conditions has stimulated the imagination to picture every kind of Utopia, but evolutionary, not revolutionary, change is our chosen theme, so we take society as we find it—in cities, towns, and open country.

In cities we find amenities and services not achievable elsewhere, but we also find social chaos and degeneration. We would like to cause the city to grow from a chaos to a cosmos by recognizing human dependence upon community organization. We would like to divide the city into neighborhoods, providing their citizens with self-government, with education and recreation, with some morale-building institution like the church—and where possible, with industry and commerce. The strongest and most potent element in an environment is *morale*.

In brief, we would strive for a complete community small enough for its citizens to form a cohering body politic. The bees are our model. When their hive grows unwieldy they divide it into two separate communities.

This model for the city is at present realized to a certain extent in towns, and we should plan to strengthen and complete it.

In the open country another point of view dominates. It is proper that a portion of our population should be protected in their desire to live among the surroundings that nature provides, and to enjoy some freedom from human intrusions and some opportunity for meditation and self-renewal.

Quae cum ita sint, our task is to picture (1) the evolving of our city into a coordinated group of organic communities or neighborhoods, (2) the strengthening and completing of our town-unit of population, (3) the protection and encouragement of our open-country folk.*

The social unit will be stimulated and its morale improved if it is a unit visually as well as socially. It should develop an outline or boundary, and a system of its own of educational and recreational centers. More than all else it should fight against the dead-level of mediocrity caused by standardization and nationalization.

The tendency to have every shopping center in America look like every other; to produce houses by the thousand all the same, like trailers; to have mail-order lampposts and hydrants and street signs; this is not only banality—it marks the road to apathy and stultification.

The old planet is pleasing today because of the local color and customs of its various peoples. The clustered tile-roofed houses overhanging the shores of the Mediterranean are totally and fascinatingly different from the dwellings of Marblehead, and these again from Rotterdam; and that is salvation. It means local pride, and gives to each community a soul or ethos of its own.

This is an age of experimentation. Let each community insist on its own quest for a visual basis of charm and delight.

There is enough ennui from infinite repetition of the same auto, the same fedora, the same standard store front. Where local architecture can be encouraged it will leaven the lump of conformity. It is in the towns that we find whatever there is of encouragement along these lines. Many towns do deliberately encourage and preserve a distinctive atmosphere and lay down for themselves a "manifest destiny." This tends to keep citizens *in* the community and therefore to create a soil for indigenous ideas, and a local expression of them.

To permit our schools to indoctrinate architectural stu-

* Compare Mr. Morgan's plan for "little wildernesses" (p. 144) with Mr. Greeley's "open-country folk." It is doubtful if isolated agrarian workers have any more "opportunity for meditation and self-renewal" than urban dwellers. Compare also Theodore McCrosky's comments (p. 140) on the dangers of a town-unit culture.—Ed.

dents in a single mode of expression is stupid and deadly. Architecture should interpret, not indoctrinate. History shows architectural evolution *without a break* from Egypt to Saskatchewan.

In the open country conservation of what is provided by nature comes first. Modification of the scene by man must be at a minimum, or at least in harmony with the preponderant note of nature.

THE DEMOCRATIC SPIRIT IN ARCHITECTURE

BY ARTHUR E. MORGAN

Without attempting to be precise in his conclusions, Mr. Morgan points in the following paper to the new possibilities inherent in a truly democratic architecture. Arthur E. Morgan was born in Ohio in 1878. He holds honorary degrees from the University of Colorado, the University of North Carolina, and Antioch College. After practicing as an engineer both in a government position and in private practice (he is still president of the Dayton Morgan Engineering Company), he became president of Antioch College and served there from 1920 to 1936. He is best known for the outstanding job he did as chairman of the Tennessee Valley Authority between 1933 and 1938.

The simplicity which Contreras and Greeley visualize in today's architecture, in the two preceding papers, takes on additional meaning when Morgan contrasts our democratic environment with the "grandeur, dominance, and power" which architecture interpreted in previous periods.

ANY discipline or tradition, such as architecture, medicine, engineering, or business, tends to provide for itself a pattern or frame of reference by which it judges itself and justifies itself. Sometimes such discipline or traditions undertake to declare the independence of the particular tradition from the sum total of human discipline and tradition.

Thus we have the standard of "art for art's sake," implying that a work of art should be judged solely for its esthetic merit, and not by any other standard, such as economic or ethical. Similarly we have the doctrine, "business is business," which implies that business should be judged by its effectiveness for achieving its own end—profit—and not by any other standards, such as ethical or esthetic.

Such doctrines are fundamentally untenable because they tend to make human efforts cancel each other out rather than to act together for providing human satisfaction. If a work of art has unethical implications (I use the word "unethical" rather than "immoral" because the latter implies the authority of usage whereas the former implies inherent economy and value in human relationships), the fact that it has esthetic quality does not relieve it from valid criticism. If it makes inordinate drain on the limited social resources from which all human needs must find satisfaction, then it is not immune from criticism because it is esthetically excellent. Similarly, if business conduct is unesthetic or unethical, it is not excused just because it makes a profit. Where these limited standards prevail great additional effort is required in order to overcome the ugliness or the unethical conduct of business, or to bear the undue economic burdens or counteract the degenerating influence of art, and the over-all economy and satisfaction of life is reduced. Every valid need of the human spirit should be satisfied in such a way as not to infringe on the satisfactions of other human needs.

This principle applies to architecture. That art is not sound unless it is in harmony with other ways of meeting human needs. It must have consideration for the limitations of total human resources, and not call for more than its suitable share; it must have respect for the ethical integrity of human life, for cultural, social, and personal needs. Architecture must be a part of the effort to see life whole.

In its origins architecture was the servant of royalty, nobility, and power. The impressions sought to be conveyed were grandeur, dominance, and power. Somewhat as beautiful etchings on a fine sword might give it distinction without interfering with its chief use, so sheer beauty in architecture may have been subordinate to expression of power and prestige.

When architecture came to serve democracy, the influence of this background did not quickly disappear. As the people took over the functions of the king, they imitated his attitudes, and architecture was their servant. Official American architecture illustrates this condition. In two centuries the democratic spirit has made headway in America, in architecture as elsewhere, but escape from the undemocratic spirit of the past is far from complete.

Full acceptance of the democratic spirit in architecture, as in other phases of life, would have revolutionary results. Architecture and the related arts would be refined and ennobled by such a liberation. Prestige, as a competitive status, would be displaced. Friends do not seek prestige among themselves. Democratic architecture will be modest. It will seek integration with its environment, not dominance over it.

One essential element of freedom is freedom from unnecessary economic burdens. The old architecture was a burden-maker, with small consideration for the burden-bearer. Democratic architecture will have a keen sense of social responsibility. In view of the enormous burdens which society must bear to achieve a good life, democratic architecture will not promote expenditures in its own field that are not in good proportion to other social needs and possibilities. It will not exceed its best share of the social budget.

Partly as a discipline of his own attitude, the democratic architect will not tolerate compensation on the basis of a percentage of expenditures incurred. Were not this practice deeply imbedded in custom, and did it not make possible the statement of large fees in innocently small figures, the custom would be seen for what it is—highly unethical. It is unethical because it creates a sharp and unnecessary conflict between the interest of the architect and that of his

client. For him to make unusual effort to achieve economies and so to reduce costs, or to achieve exceptional quality through fine design, is for him not only to be unpaid for
such productive service, but often to be penalized for it
by reduction of compensation for his success in achieving
economies. The profession of architecture suffers griev-
ously from this unethical custom. In many respects transition to the temper of democracy is a vague concept, difficult
to take hold of. Here is a specific matter in which architecture can measure its ethical vigor. Compensation measured
by work done rather than by expenses incurred would have
a refining influence on architecture, and on architects.

WHEN WE KNOW MAN,
THEN WE CAN PLAN

BY ERNEST J. KUMP

After the calm statements preceding, Ernest Kump's insistence
that we cannot begin to plan until we really know the people
we are planning for is an almost angry reminder that "despite
all our high-sounding proclamations and elaborate promises,
our planning so far has failed."

Mr. Kump, an architect with an extensive practice in California, is best known for advances in school planning and construction. His experiments in classroom lighting, as well as the
design and marketing of prefabricated school units, have contributed much to the integration of good design with technological possibilities.

In the following paper Kump punctures what might become
a smug assumption that we know best the sort of physical environment man needs. We can't be sure, he insists, until "we
know man a good deal better than we have thus far demonstrated."

ARCHITECTURE is an art and not a science. Architecture fails to fulfill its true purpose whenever and wherever
it views and conducts itself as a science rather than an art.

Today, because of a deteriorating sense of values, we are

permitting what is only a means to an end to be taken as the end itself. Today, because of confusion in our thinking, we are allowing the servant to rule the master. Art should envision and prescribe the goal. Science's only role is to help attain that goal. Art is the end. Science is only a means to the end. Much of our current trouble comes from putting the cart before the horse.

The more that architecture considers itself a science, the less it will be able to perform as an art. And the less it functions as an art, the more it will fail to create the environment man requires, not only for happiness but for actual survival.

This is not "one world" because of science; because the radio and airplane have abridged time and distance. This is one world because all men survive through order and perish through disorder.

More than three centuries ago the poet, John Donne, said: "No man is an Iland, intire of it selfe; every man is a peece of the continent, a part of the maine; . . . any man's death diminishes me, because I am involved in Mankinde. And therefore never send to know for whom the bell tolls; it tolls for thee."

Architecture is "involved in Mankinde." It is involved in mankind because it is charged with the duty of providing man with a portion of that cosmic order in his environment which he must have or perish. And architecture cannot perform that duty as long as it views man as merely an economic unit, as a statistic in total population, as merely a functional creature requiring so many square feet of shelter from the elements. Architecture cannot succeed in achieving its full purpose as long as it believes, as science would have it, that man can live by bread alone.

Architecture is honored by having delegated to it the tremendously important assignment of planning man's physical environment. But it will never do so successfully until it first knows man. *When we know man, then we can plan!* And we will never know man, as long as we believe he can be fully evaluated by the test tube and the tape measure.

The successful planning of man's physical environment means knowing man not only as factory worker, artisan, merchant, doctor, clergyman, professor—as earner and spender—but man also as husband, father, brother; as poet, philosopher, painter, dreamer; man as spirit as well as body; *man as a whole*. And we, as architects, shall never know man as a whole until we discard the narrow, particularizing, separating view of science, and take the broad, unifying view of art.

Then, viewing man as a *whole being*, and, realizing his total requirements, we can go from the general to the particular. Not until we, as artists, are able to *see man whole* can we, as architects, succeed in planning his physical environment.

Despite all our high-sounding proclamations and elaborate promises, our planning so far has failed. It will continue to fail, despite all our conferences and other manifestations of good intention until we, as architects, discard the Procrustean idea that man is made for planners and realize, rather, that *planners are made for man*.

After we have seen the whole; after we have mastered the general; then we can safely study particulars and deal with the parts that combine and unify to make the whole. Processes, materials, techniques—these are important, and have their place. But they are details more or less incidental; and in the hands of the *real* architect, they will take their proper place at his command. Today many of us, instead of commanding them, are being commanded by them with consequences that are bound to ensue when we allow the horse to usurp the driver's place.

Concerning our attitude toward all these functional processes, materials, techniques, etc.—all these details—perhaps it would pay us to reflect on the words of Christ, who said: "Seek ye first the Kingdom of God . . . and all these things shall be added unto you."

To the architect seriously concerned with seeing architecture assume its true role and achieve its true purpose, the "Kingdom of God," as related to architecture, should not be too difficult to locate nor to bound and describe. Actually, gaining it may be another matter. But at least we can seek, which is what we are enjoined to do, and what we are promised will assure us that all these other things will be added unto us. When architecture seeks ardently and uncompromisingly for fundamentals, incidentals will take care of themselves.

It might, I fear, carry us beyond the time limits of this Conference to attempt full discussion and agreement concerning *all* the fundamentals embraced in "Planning Man's Physical Environment." However, there is one fundamental on which, I believe, we can all agree. That is man. Unless and until we *know* man—know him in his wholeness and completeness—all of our planning will give him ashes for beauty, and make his last state worse than his first. For the principles of architecture, as of all art, are bound up inextricably with the laws of life; and the soul of man is a thousand times more sensitive to changes of interpretation in the world about him than is the barometer to changes in its surrounding atmosphere.

Who knows, for a certainty, what is best for man, or what he really wants? Who knows, for a certainty, that he wants to live in a scientifically planned community? Despite all its functional advantages—near-by schools, churches, theaters, parks, playgrounds, supermarket and community center, and quiet streets safe from the hazards of motor traffic—despite all this, suppose he just doesn't like it?

Remembering that our children so often spurn the manufactured toy, with its scientific perfection and synthetic beauty, for some clumsy but homemade contraption, and desert the safe public playground with its scientifically planned and supervised recreation, for the self-expression of dodging motor cars on a busy street—remembering this, perhaps we should ask ourselves if man may not require something in his physical environment that scientific deductions cannot determine.

I do not say we should not plan. But, until we know man a good deal better than we have thus far demonstrated— should we not go slow in reaching anything like irrevocable decisions concerning *mass* planning of his physical environment?

I do not, let me repeat, suggest that we abandon planning. But I do urge that before we go too far in our efforts to plan man's physical environment, we be more certain than I believe we now can be, that we know what we are doing. That we *know* this man for whom we are to plan. And, I say again in closing, that we can only know him when we view him as artists, not scientists; when, in other words, *we see him whole!*

When we know Man, then we can Plan!

THE DESIGNER AS A COMMON MAN

BY RICHARD M. BENNETT

The final paper in this section is a rather calm answer to Kump's plea that we must study man. Richard Bennett, member of the Chicago firm of planners and architects, Loebl, Schlossman & Bennett, former professor of architecture at Yale, replies in effect that architects *are* men. The need, he says, is an identification of the planner with the people he plans for.

IT WAS Francis Bacon who proposed a scientific era in which society and matter were to be studied until we finally understood the form of things. He thought that only then would the world have the raw material on which men could decide about a desirable Utopia. It almost seems as if that time of decision is now here. Men are everywhere more concerned with what they will do with the world than they are with any further examinations of the parts into which they have broken it. This ultimate synthesis is the real problem of the Princeton meeting.

We are indebted to the nineteenth century for the idea of a functional architecture, an architecture which must first of all recognize the purpose for our constructions. When we think in terms of the larger environment, then we must first of all concern ourselves with common purpose, for here lies the root of our solution.

The artist and the designer will find it fruitless to continue to dispute existing methods and present solutions. Scientific consumer research will discover no common purposes—only common acceptances of what is. The common purpose can be found, or will be found, when the artist and designer again recognizes himself as a common man and realizes that his desires and his intuition lie in every man, no matter how dormant.

Professing democracy, recent generations have been taught to exalt the differences between men: to isolate, scrutinize, and exalt the fraction that makes one personality spectacularly different from another, forgetting the larger part which is the same in all men.

This analytical dissection reflects the concern of science with the elements and origin of our world. Today we have all the pieces.

The designer, the architect, the artist now has the task of synthesizing, to provide a plan—a vision of what the world can be. It will not be adequate if it is based on the facet he imagines makes him different from other men—his plan must be a vision which has its genesis buried deep in the hearts of all men.

SECTION II

LIMITATIONS
AND
POSSIBILITIES

INTRODUCTION

BY THOMAS H. CREIGHTON

HAVING established the fact that an architectural development must be based on contemporary man and his present-day society, the discussion now turns to those factors which limit the full satisfaction of man's environmental needs or, on the other hand, make their fulfillment possible. Although the original title given to this panel was *Physical Possibilities and Limitations of Design*, the discussion prior to, during, and after the Conference ranged through a number of limitations and opportunities which might be classed as social, economic, and political, as well as those that are purely physical. The fact was recognized immediately that the very social pattern in which we move has its limiting characteristics; every joint activity of human beings which develops into a social form inevitably imposes its own restrictions on activities formulated within its framework.

Then it became apparent that some of the physical limitations are nature's own, but many are man-made. For example, it is very difficult to distinguish the natural limitations of building materials (limitations inherent in the materials themselves as they are mined, quarried, or manufactured) from the restrictions on their use which are imposed by our social system, by custom, by transportation, and by methods of exchange. Howard Vermilya asked if it was possible to "limit the discussion to the physical possibilities and limitations of the structure," or whether it was not necessary to "include as well the physical possibilities and limitations of man and other elements such as that of our social and economic environment as they affect the structure." Arthur Holden replied:

Of course we cannot discuss these things in a vacuum and should not forget that the individual and social uses to which man puts architecture and his environment form a prime consideration. [We must consider] how man's habits, individual as well as social, have limited his development and how his increasing knowledge and understanding may help him improve his environment provided he can put his improved knowledge to increasingly better use. Of course, some of the trouble is that as man learns about new tools that he can work with, and new principles, he tends to forget some of the basic things that he knew in the past and he uses old materials and principles badly. The whole jigsaw period is evidence of this.

The primary unstated axiom, then, is that we must operate within our *existing* social structure. There is no discussion, in the papers that follow, of a possible change in that structure to remove certain limitations or develop new possibilities. Rather there is an emphasis on the point that we have not understood or taken advantage of the potentialities now open to us. To John Burchard, our great opportunity is the new social purpose and the intense social specialization of buildings today. "The distinguishing element of our time is not its materials; we have but one important new one for architecture," he says. Howard Vermilya believes that our great new possibilities are due to increased *knowledge* of materials and their synthetic use: "Materials can and are being developed to perform at higher stresses with greater uniformity and durability." For Gordon Lorimer, the need, before we can exploit full possibilities, is a fuller understanding of the increasing limitations (as well as the opening up of new possibilities) as we proceed from traditional on-site construction to full factory fabrication.

Arthur Holden feels that our great lack has been an understanding of economic limitations and possibilities. "Creative design has been hampered," he says, "because the designing professions have neglected to appreciate that their value for society must be expressed in terms of exchange and finance."

All of these attitudes, despite their differing emphases,

stress the fact that architecture of the twentieth century has not begun to develop potentials *within* the limitations of our present social, economic, and political frame. Only Richard Neutra pointed out, before the Conference itself, that "design action" can become "an instrument of broad change, in contrast to catering to existing established requirements and perpetuating a status quo." Yet Neutra at the same time made the inescapable comment that "technique is a consequence of socio-economic trends."

If this section looks back to the first one in its realization of the social understanding necessary for good design, it also looks forward to the consideration of architectural form. The question is, after all, what possibilities and limitations are there in the use of form and the planning of space. Can "design" be considered apart from, for example, economic restrictions? Richard Bennett asked, rhetorically, if the Conference could not "differentiate space planning from economic determinism, if that is the right term for economic planning that uses politics to effect regimentation." To Walter Gropius it seemed that the emphasis should be "more on coordination of all the problems involved than on this or that topic." He wrote before the Conference:

[A] great difficulty I find with the designer is to get him into the habit of thinking in a three-fold way in "space terms, in technical terms, in economic terms." Intellectually this is easily understood, but getting into the automatic habit of thinking simultaneously in these three directions, on fields which have their own laws separate from those of the other, is a rare achievement to be gained by experience.

The specific "physical limitations and possibilities" of building materials and equipment, as the elements producing architectural form, were discussed little in the formal papers, but received attention in correspondence among the participants. Henry Kamphoefner wrote:

I think that the proportions in the art form of the people as related to the materials should receive thorough investigation and study. Less than twenty years ago in most schools, and to some extent in the less progressive schools today, proportion is taught as a visual expression which often degenerates into eclecticism. If modern architecture as a socio-economic art form achieves the enclosing of the greatest amount of usable space with the least amount of material, proportion must be based on the logical and economic use of material.

George Fred Keck echoed this point of view, speaking of techniques of construction rather than individual materials. He wrote as follows:

Building technique qualifies design. By definition an architect is a "master builder." Building techniques are of first importance, design is secondary and dependent upon techniques. Louis Sullivan thought so when he said "form *follows* function." The importance of techniques has been neglected by architects. The war has not had much to do with changes in type and use of materials, except as it shakes our complacency and jolts us to newer realizations. Prefabrication is a technique of construction, and as such will affect design.

Not all the participants agreed with this point of view. Looking ahead to the discussion on the philosophy of form, Joseph Hudnut wrote in answer to Kamphoefner:

I cannot agree that "proportion must be based on the logical and economic use of materials." Of course I think that proportion is intimately related to building technique and materials and I might even go so far as to say that every material has its proper proportion, but that is not the same thing as saying that this proportion must be based on some form of logic or economic use. I am also inclined to quarrel with the assumption that good architecture is that which encloses the greatest amount of space with the least amount of material. That sounds to me like something out of Calvin.

Quite naturally, the present-day self-imposed limitation of standardization accounted for a great deal of discussion among the participants. Some thought it raised a sharp new

THOMAS H. CREIGHTON

danger; others saw it as an inevitable characteristic of our industrial society opening new environmental possibilities that we have not yet realized. Talbot Hamlin, raising the question in pre-Conference correspondence, wrote:

How best can the infinitely varying needs of today's differing individuals be taken care of in today's architecture and community design? Both technological and economic considerations have established a habit of insisting upon standardization in as many elements as possible. This trend has become a habit so strong that standardization is often imposed when no economies result from its use—it saves thought; that is all. This movement has profoundly affected architectural thinking as can be seen, for instance, in Le Corbusier's concept of city planning, much of the work of CIAM, and outstandingly in the design of many government housing developments.

This alarmed view is balanced by Walter Gropius's insistence (page 43) that we must work for standardized parts rather than standardized buildings, a point of view which he feels would open new possibilities rather than impose additional limitations, through making possible "diversity within unity."

In any event, there was general acceptance of the fact that architects can no longer afford to hide from the reality of factory manufacture of materials or ignore the possibilities (granted the limitations) of partial or complete prefabrication. The aspect of the matter which produced a basic conflict, continuing on through other sections of the discussion (i.e., Ralph Walker's paper on page 76 and Talbot Hamlin's on page 209) was whether man or the machine is master. In other words, are the limitations so great that we must accept design products that are really bad *except for* simplicity of manufacture, or are the possibilities so great that we can turn them to an advantage that man never before had in controlling his environment? The only conclusion that one can draw from the discussion of

· 31 ·

this point is that it is up to the designers to discover the advantages by recognizing the limitations.

The most constructive theme in this section, recurring through many papers and remarks, is the call for proper research, so that there can be a scientific basis for determining just what the limitations and possibilities in our present time consist of. John Burchard speaks harshly when he says, "It is childish to play with science and to talk of insolation, sound, light, in terms which a freshman physicist would reject as untrue." Howard Vermilya is not so pessimistic about the research that has been accomplished; he points to better understanding of materials, to studies in thermal conductivity of materials, studies of sound, light, color. Yet Richard Bennett, writing before the Conference, echoed somewhat Burchard's point of view:

An institute of research for the profession of architecture is tragically needed—the scientific method is not being used in our profession. The scientific approach is not that of teaching boys an extra year of math or science they will never use, but for our profession the scientific method must be developed to bring together related information obscured by traditional methods and modern pseudo-science.

Lawrence Kocher put his finger on the sort of research that most of the discussants were thinking of; in pre-Conference correspondence he called for coordination of "technical" building studies with sociological and other scientific research. He wrote:

It is probable that we should take steps to coordinate building research, planning, design, and construction. Research is the foundation for the development of new solutions—not alone for materials, but for living, for planning, for social relationships. This research should be a coordinated endeavor of the architect, the town planner, the engineer, the specialists in biology, sociology, psychology, and so on.

The remarks that follow represent many diverse points of view. They seem agreed on several things: We must take full advantage of the possibilities in design which our industrialized society offers; we must recognize and work within the limitations that society imposes; to do this we must work in secure knowledge, not guess, rationalize, or hypothesize, else, as John Burchard says, "we shall be found out, and quickly."

PROFESSIONAL LIMITATIONS
AND POSSIBILITIES

BY JOHN E. BURCHARD

The chairman of this section of the Conference, John Ely Burchard, was born in Minnesota in 1898. Through his career he has been associated with architecture in an advisory and critical capacity. His interests and activities have been varied and penetrating, as one might assume from his present positions as Director of Libraries at the Massachusetts Institute of Technology, Chairman of the Board of Publications of the same institution, Director of the Albert Farwell Bemis Foundation, and member of the Advisory Council of the Department of Physics at Princeton. Recently he has been a professional advisor on library programs to Rice Institute, New York University, and the United Nations.

The position that Mr. Burchard establishes in the following paper is one of challenge to the designing professions. Their technical pretensions, their social unawareness, even their professional journals come under scrutiny. Finally he asks if they intend to face up to their responsibilities and make of modern architecture something important. No one else, he points out, can make that decision.

THERE was a time to clean the stables; a time to shock; a time to argue. The last was a long time. All these times are over for modern architecture. There remains only the time for decision. Is this thing a mere style; will it some day have become a tradition?

The great figures, many of whom are here, did the stable cleaning. They reaffirmed the axioms. They did everything necessary to shock. They argued brilliantly. There are no more axioms to state. To shock is no longer necessary, not even desirable. Perpetually to make something new may call fleeting attention to one's self, may capture the ephemeral applause of a self-admiring claque; but it is not a panacea for progress. There are times for advance; there are times for consolidation, times of more achievement if less spectacle. The same thing applies to the forum. The *avant-garde* and the reactionary alike mouth their controversies to empty benches.

The distinguishing element of our time is not its materials; we have but one important new one for architecture and cost rejects the full exploitation of the theoretical potentials of structural steel and aluminum. The distinguishing element is neither economic nor political. There have been fascist and communist architectures ere this and they are alike for the simple reason that they are official. Some democratic architecture may be unofficial, but this too has occurred before.

The great distinction of today is that we ask that more classes of people be well served by our buildings; we demand for every building a degree of specialization hitherto unknown. It is presumptuous for any architect now to build a terminus, a hospital, a school, a merchandise mart, without sober consideration of the technical requirements; presumptuous for him to assume that he can define them a priori; presumptuous for him to think that he knows more about them than the technician who uses them.*

• Writing to Arthur Holden before the Conference, Burchard elaborated this point as follows: "The great social demands of today for hospitals, schools, housing groups, transportation terminals, distribution and recreational centers, power complexes (TVA), are the spur to whatever is in the long run to be significant in our architecture. Whether the office building was ever a comparable spur in an earlier day is debatable; but surely the church and the hospice were in the Middle Ages; the temple, the agora, and the theater in classic times.

"The human needs are probably in the large not too different, but "the extension of the technical requirements is of another order of magnitude. This poses the sharp problem whether a man who is competent to design a temple (fully competent) can conceivably be fully competent to design

So today the architect is designer at the end and not at the beginning. He must first of all be an interviewer, an objective recorder of needs, an understanding examiner of techniques. This process may well take longer than the final synthesis, the space arrangement, which is the design.

There is risk that modern architecture does not follow its own precepts. It is no more noble to preconceive a building with a special structure and then force everything to fit, than it is to preconceive it in the mold of St. Trophime. Flexibility as a fetish can lead to amorphism. It is childish to play with science and to talk of insolation, sound, light, in terms which a freshman physicist would reject as untrue. These things are not emotions and pseudo-scientific treatment of them as emotions simply will not do. We shall be found out, and quickly.

It is possible that all the architecture necessary for a scientific time can be created by intuition, but if this be true let us stop prating about modern technology and applied research; if it be not true, then let us look coldly at our professional literature, the worst supplied to any profession in the world. What first-rate doctor, chemist, or barrister could grow in his profession without assiduous cultivation of his professional journals? Who of us could honestly assert our world would be much changed if the postman stopped bringing all our professional magazines? We can no longer be content in architectural journalism to limit our scope to remarks about bistros, personalities, fees, unification, to gossip about the Washington bureaus, to pictures of so-called important monuments printed upside down for the greater titillation, to wit, in the form of letters to the editor, or to swoon in mutual admiration. We need fiber in our documents and not pap; for a time this

---

or even to coordinate the designers of a great broadcasting center. The difference between the two comparable elements in the Greek state was as great philosophically but much less great technically, and the same spirit might be able to touch both with his genius. Perhaps he still can, but what to do about this question is perhaps the foremost one facing architecture. Can the architect, for example, properly be the master planner of city or region at all?"—Ed.

may require us to employ technical translators; but if we will give these translations our ears and our eyes we shall in the long run be able to dispense with them. American physicists, chemists, and biologists have an analogous contemporary problem since few of them can read Russian. They are not so stupid as to pretend they understand a language which it is essential for them truly to comprehend. We can afford a comparable humility.

We will do well, then, in this time of decision to ask ourselves whether we profess more than we practice. If we do not practice what we profess, all will be lost. It is time for critical self-scrutiny.

Do we really survey the technical need without prejudice; do we refrain from imposing our own clichés; do we avoid facile rationalization and the pseudo-scientific; are we prepared to bring humanism to the mechanism we have already prescribed with such authority? These are not rhetorical questions; only the thoughtless could answer with a chorused "yes."

This is the time for decision. The next few years will decide whether modern architecture is an important landmark in world history or an unimportant and transient style. Ours is the choice.

THE NEED FOR RESEARCH

BY HOWARD P. VERMILYA

In the paper that follows, Howard Vermilya provides a transition between Burchard's challenge to the profession of designers and the succeeding discussions of more specific limitations and possibilities. While he lists many fields in which study has opened up new possibilities of design and defined the limitations which face the designer in the way of known needs and available materials, Vermilya concludes with an appeal for additional research which is at least as compelling as Burchard's, and perhaps more pointed.

IN A limited space it seems wise to restrict ourselves to a discussion of those physical limitations of design over which man has control, and to consider these only in their broadest sense.

We must accept the forces of nature—cold, heat, wind, rain, light, darkness, gravity, and chemical and physical reactions. These limitations have challenged architects from the beginning. With each increase in our knowledge and understanding, the level of physical design has been raised.

Nature's own materials have placed limitations upon design. Increased knowledge of materials and of the engineering of their use has enlarged the physical possibilities of design. Today through synthetic processes materials can and are being developed to perform at higher stresses with greater uniformity and durability. The synthetic approach lends itself to the development of composite materials of the sandwich type. Research in adhesives, in welding techniques, and in concrete have made possible the use of slabs or panels as well as other structural forms with their more effective stress distribution, permitting the use of lighter and (in terms of materials used) more economical sections.

Understanding of the physiology of man has introduced new limitations in the sense that we no longer feel free to do things that we know are contrary to physical requirements. At the same time it has increased our awareness of the need for a higher level of attainment and the possibilities, through design, of improving man's comfort. Studies of the thermal properties of materials and the principles of heat transfer as they affect design through the choice of materials and heating equipment are opening up new possibilities in terms of comfort. Studies of sound and its absorption or transmission are at the same time increasing the limitations and possibilities of design. Studies of natural and artificial light in relation to better seeing are affecting design in efforts to provide an abundance of light as well as to eliminate glare and contrast. Studies of fatigue as they relate to sound and light are also significant. Studies of color in relation to light absorption and the use of color for accident prevention are further instances of the results of an understanding of man's physiology and its influence on design.

Legislative regulation of buildings as contained in building codes, zoning, and other ordinances designed to protect the health, safety, and general welfare of society are one of the severest limitations under which design must operate. The severity lies in their rigidity and not in their legitimate purposes. The hope for relief lies in the possibility of phrasing these standards in terms of performance or function. It lies further in the selection of administrators who are capable of interpretation of performance standards.

Underlying each group of limitations which has been mentioned there lies the possibility that through research our understanding may be broadened and design given greater scope. Today society suffers largely through the maldistribution of the benefits it can bestow upon man. Dependence must be placed on research if we are, through design, to bestow more broadly the benefits of which architecture is capable. One instance of possible benefits from research is in the field of housing, where few can afford an adequate standard. Research leading to reduced costs in this field is essential. In other fields, buildings as a capital cost item affect the price of everything we use and consume. Not only can research lead to reduced costs, but it may be directed to produce a higher level of design through a better understanding of the objectives and mediums of design.

LIMITATIONS AND POSSIBILITIES OF BUILDING TECHNIQUES

BY A. GORDON LORIMER

Born and educated in Scotland, Gordon Lorimer has become known nationally for his work on and advocacy of dimensional coordination of building products and the "modular" construction which can result. Several years ago he gave up his position as Chief Architect in the Department of Public Works in New York City, and established practice for himself while acting as Technical Consultant to the Producers' Council.

Analyzing the benefits and limitations of various building techniques as they move from traditional on-site methods to complete prefabrication, Lorimer points to the close relationship between these construction methods and two other important factors: economic influences and labor.

THOUGH the approach is somewhat over-simplified, *production*, the most important segment of the building cycle, may be subdivided into four methods, all of which are being used at least to some extent at the present time, with a nebulous line separating each one from the one following.

1. TRADITIONAL. This is direct field construction using commonly available materials. The materials are adjusted and fitted by artisans to specific design dimensions prescribed by the architect. Special shop drawing and individual fabrication of most elements, such as stairs, are necessary.

Benefits: Great design flexibility to meet individual requirements.

Limitations: High cost of job labor, governed particularly by the efficiency and output of the individual worker.

2. TRADITIONAL BUILDING, PLUS ORGANIZED JOB PREFABRICATION OF REPETITIVE PARTS. Site prefabrication of large elements of the building can be accomplished by organizing the design to permit repetitive structural components.

Benefits: Labor economy and job speed.

Limitations: Construction is subject to vagaries of weather, or cost of creating temporary shelter.

Design is disciplined, but only to the extent that this fact is usually beneficial rather than detrimental.

3. UNIT FABRICATION AT OFF-SITE PLANT. In this method

field operation is limited to the assembly of factory-made elements, or other assemblies of considerable size.

Benefits: Economy derived from volume production under controlled conditions.

Limitations: Design is limited to scale of units and to material selected by fabricator.

4. COMPLETE FACTORY FABRICATION.

Benefits: Controlled line production with attendant economies.

Limitations: The economies are possible only if full demand and continuous operation are maintained.

In time, economic need for amortization of equipment may result in persistence of outmoded design.

If one visualizes the construction operation as a circle, there are two other large segments in addition to production: they are *economic influences* and *labor*.

The economic segment merges with the production segment in the selection of the means of distribution and the financing of the project. If the circle is swung around by movement of the construction trend as it veers toward prefabrication, the economic segment moves with it, and in turn reaches new possibilities and new limitations. Most important is the fact that a whole new phase of marketing appears; the distribution and sale of building products—materials and equipment—as well as the sale of land and marketing of the completed structure become processes quite different from those needed for traditional on-site construction.

In the same way labor swings with the rest of the circle and finds itself facing a new set of conditions. Building labor is still largely divided on an individual craft union basis, rigidly compartmentalized. Many restraints have already been placed on product and assembly development as a result of this situation. As the trend increases toward off-site fabrication there becomes evident a great need for a new building labor classification. There must emerge the skilled assembly mechanic, not restricted in his work to any one material. This may require a vertical union arrangement, with the economic incentive of a guaranteed annual wage. Before we can estimate the limitations to full exploitation of the newer construction techniques which the readjustment of labor conditions may impose, we will have to find out the answers to several questions:

In what way can the present craft union approach to high wages through "scarcity" be changed to the concept of high annual wages through large volume and continued productivity?

What would be the long-term demand for building labor if high productivity can be made effective?

Thus it is apparent that there are design limitations which arise as we move from traditional methods of construction to the new techniques made possible by industrialization. What is not so generally recognized, however, is that equally great social and economic limitations appear in the related fields of economics and labor. Unless they are all solved at the same time, the designers of man's physical environment will not be able to take full advantage of all the possibilities that should be open to them and to the society they plan for.

PREFABRICATION:
A FREEDOM FROM LIMITATIONS

BY WALTER GROPIUS

One of the most distinguished architects and one of the outstanding educators of our time, Dr. Gropius has been Chairman of the Graduate School of Design at Harvard since 1937. He is perhaps best known as an architect for the new buildings which he designed for the Bauhaus Institute when that school moved to Dessau in 1926, although he had already accomplished much work in Germany before then, and has been responsible for a number of projects since, in England and the United States. When he was called to reorganize the Weimar School of Art after the first World War, into what became the influential Bauhaus, Gropius had an opportunity to put into practice his theories of architectural education which, briefly, are based on a belief that it is necessary "to avert mankind's enslavement by the machine by giving its products a content of significance and reality, and so saving the home from mechanistic anarchy." At the Bauhaus and at Harvard, Gropius has insisted that his students understand industrial processes and construction techniques, so that their designs should be adapted to contemporary limitations and possibilities.

In the following paper, Dr. Gropius makes a plea once more for this understanding, specifically pointing his argument to the solution of the social problem of inadequate housing. The limitations which Lorimer pointed out in the preceding paper, as we move from complete on-site construction to factory fabrication, seem small to Gropius in comparison to the social benefits.

WE OFTEN find that people are sceptical as to whether the great need for shelter can be solved at all by mass fabrication of homes or whether we should even be willing to accept the spirit of mass production in the one great sector of modern existence which has so far successfully resisted it.

Surely we are fearful that mass production of homes, while striving for economic standardization, may harmfully affect the legitimate requirements of the individual. But why should we cast away the good with the bad? Human inventiveness will eventually overcome transitional shortcomings and will live up to the task of combining industrial standardization with manifold flexibility of use. For the true aim of prefabrication is certainly not the dull multiplication of a housetype *ad infinitum*; men will always rebel against attempts at overmechanization which are contrary to life. But industrialization will not stop at the threshold of building. We have no other choice but to accept the challenge of the machine in all fields of production until men finally adapt it fully to serve their biological needs.

People still look at prefabrication as an entirely revolutionary idea, but it has proved to be a slow evolutionary movement and should not be expected to throw the building market out of gear. Is not the brick a prefabricated unit? Very gradually the process of building is splitting up into shop production of building parts on the one hand, and site assembly of such parts on the other. More and more the tendency develops to prefabricate component parts of buildings rather than whole houses.* Here is where the emphasis belongs! The competing building industries will agree upon a reduced number of standard sizes for component parts of buildings, of wall-floor-and-roof-panels, windows, and doors. Preparatory work to simplify dimensions in the building industry is now being done by the American Standards Association. The future architect and builder will have at their disposal something like a box of blocks to play with, an infinite variety of interchangeable, machine-made parts for building which will be bought in the competitive market and be assembled into individual buildings of different appearances and sizes. Prefabrication, as a logical progressive process, aimed at raising the standard of building, will finally lead to higher quality for lower prices. There are many analogous cases of industry successfully offering improved commodities at lesser prices to serve as evidence for such a statement.

* There has been a tendency on the part of some writers recently to regard the point of view which Dr. Gropius expresses (prefabrication of parts rather than whole houses) a compromise or a backing down from the original arguments of those who have been advocating prefabrication for many years. This is not so in Gropius' case. In his book, *The New Architecture and the Bauhaus* (Museum of Modern Art, 1918) he said: "The repetition of standardized parts, and the use of identical materials in different buildings, will have the same sort of sobering and coordinating effect on the aspects of our towns as uniformity of type in modern attire has in social life. But that will in no sense restrict the architect's freedom of design. For although every house and every block of flats will bear the unmistakable impress of our age, there will always remain, as in the clothes we wear, sufficient scope for the individual to find expression for his own personality. The net result should be a happy architectonic combination of maximum standardization and maximum variety."—Ed.

Prefabrication will thus become a vital instrument to solve the housing problem economically.

Adequate shelter is a basic need of the population. In our serious housing emergency we cannot afford to disregard for sentimental reasons any potential means for successful relief. The housing shortage is not like the sugar shortage, a mere consequence of the war. The housing shortage has developed gradually during the period of industrialization just because the machine did not penetrate far enough into the large and complex field of the production of buildings. For example, in 1937 the average cost of a family dwelling had increased to 193 per cent of its 1913 cost, according to the Bureau of Labor Statistics, whereas the average cost of an automobile had simultaneously decreased to 60 per cent of its 1913 price. The increasing cost of labor involved had almost doubled the cost of building during the same period that the price of the machine-made automobile was nearly halved.

The fact that hand labor is still necessary in building (coupled with other factors such as inefficiency in management) has resulted in failure to keep the price for dwellings on a level with the average income. Today the average man cannot afford to purchase a decent dwelling in the free market. He buys food, clothing, and other daily goods at prices adapted to his income without any public subsidy, but the dwelling he may obtain is only an obsolete structure once built for wealthier people. Thus the government has been forced to provide subsidies. Experience prior to the last war showed that an average subsidy in the neighborhood of one hundred dollars per year was necessary to house a family fairly decently in a public housing development. If the public has to pay so high a penalty for each low-income class dwelling, we certainly need incentives to increase private enterprise. For subsidies do not lead to a real solution of the housing problem. They are to be considered only as a measure of transition until means and ways are found for solving the housing problem economically.

There is no doubt that increasingly refined methods of prefabrication will gradually reduce the price of houses and will provide vital help to free us from the hamstrings of perennial subsidies and from the governmental control and red tape that they necessarily imply. For the present transitional crisis, however, public encouragement is badly needed to help prefabrication come of age. The vast amount of publicly financed research in aviation and agriculture has promoted unprecedented progress; the same must be done for housing. The authoritative support given to prefabrication by the administration of Housing Expediter Wilson Wyatt under President Truman will probably prove to have been a beneficial step in the right direction, and results will be felt in the near future; but since Wyatt was forced to resign this help has ceased. In June 1944, the Kilgore Bill was presented to Congress "to provide for Technical Research and Studies in Housing," but it was shelved. A new and similar chance to promote the necessary research in housing, offered within the Taft-Ellender-Wagner Bill, should not again pass unheeded.

Although it is true that at present very little is available on the prefabrication market which can supersede the conventionally built house from the point of view of price and quality, we are ready for rapid progress. Increasing turnover will soon bring a change, since substantial capital, public and private, has been invested in prefabrication during the recent years.

Prefabrication must be encouraged for the ultimate social good. The coming generation will certainly blame us if we fail to overcome those understandable, though sentimental, reactions against it. We must be determined to let the human element become the dominant factor, by making prefabrication flexible enough to fulfill legitimate individual requirements. Considered in this way it is a logical progressive means to pull us out of the painful housing emergency.

MACHINE ENERGY:
THE TECHNIQUE OF OUR TIME

BY KONRAD WACHSMANN

In his career Mr. Wachsmann has been most attentive to the techniques made possible by contemporary industrial development. His prefabricated house system (General Panel Corporation, now in production on the West Coast) was developed in consultation with Walter Gropius by studying the joint relationship between vertical and horizontal panels. More recently he has perfected, with the aid of the engineer Paul Weidlinger, a steel pipe structural frame system (Mobilar Structures) which has attracted wide attention. Again, the jointing is most important in his design.

It is reasonable, then, that Wachsmann emphasizes the need in any age to understand the technical possibilities inherent in that age's control of energy, and that he points to *today's* possibilities in terms of machine-made, standardized "elements," with the joining together of these parts a matter of prime importance.

THE physical possibilities and limitations of design can be understood and analyzed if we think in terms of the energy we control and apply in order to create things. In our time that energy is electricity; it comes under our control in the form of machines, which require entirely new forms of economic progress. Application of machines means mass production. Mass production in turn imposes limitations on design, but it also makes possible the development and the use of new materials which could not be produced by the limited energy of manpower.

Mass production also results in standardization. The use of standard parts is not new; the brick is a product of standardization. Today we have progressed beyond the stage of bricks as a basic standard for building our environment. In consequence of the application of the new source of energy, we have to approach our design problems in a different way. The machine is a result of scientific research.

Therefore the building element as a product of the machine will be the result of scientific research.

The use of standardized parts is affected by the flexibility of the joint relationship. In the creation of any kind of structure, the joint between parts seems to be the most decisive factor. I remember the ceiling painting in the Sistine Chapel in Rome in which, as the central figure, Michelangelo painted God creating man. The hand of God and the hand of Adam are about to join. Around this basic body relationship are created and invented all the other uncounted combinations of relationships. This abstract picture expresses beautifully the very first step. *In the beginning is the joint.* The machine as the creator of the product permitted the introduction of the most complicated joints necessary. Since they are executed by machine, they can become more economical than a simple saw cut that is made by man. The chain of development of a structure will eventually form the following sequence:

1. The source of energy.
2. The material to be used.
3. The standard elements as finished products.
4. The system of the combinations and possibilities (in three dimensions) to fit the vertical and horizontal elements to each other.

The *joint* relationship of the mass produced elements thus becomes the all-important keypoint.

Industrialization of building construction will, therefore, be an important step in the development of man's physical environment. Any design of a modern building has to be based on such principles. If we cut a section through the wall of a so-called conventional building constructed in wood, and if we do the same with one of the so-called modern wood buildings, we would not be likely to find any difference between the two sections. The surface appearance of the "modern" house has been changed, but the core is still the same. It is not truly a modern building.

Here is another example. I recently saw again Sainte

Chappelle in Paris—one of the most remarkable of the Gothic structures. The beauty of this composition in stone and glass has always been the cause of a most unusual sensation to me. This time, although the stained glass windows had not been replaced since the war and the interior was cold, with too much contrast between light and shadow the structure yet remained grandiose and impressive. It was because of its wonderful construction, based on a skill, which has never been surpassed, in joining the elements.

These two examples—the house built today which ignores today's peculiar techniques, and the church built in the thirteenth century which fully utilized the techniques available at that time—are mentioned to illustrate again the basic principle of design which has been stated so often. It is that the planning of man's physical environment has to be based on the best use of the available technique, which in turn is based on our knowledge of and our ability to control energy; in other words, on our economy and our science. Only when it uses such means can a building, in any age, be called modern.

Anybody who is able to *improve* such methods, even in abstract terms, is indeed an artist. In our time great progress has been made. We have established the fact that a load-bearing frame can carry the building, relieving vertical surfaces from all duties other than for visual, acoustic, insulating, and insolating purposes. A new architectural development is now possible. Lightness will be the main expression of our environment. Uncounted combinations of surface elements will create our surrounding world. Precision, quality, efficiency, and economy will be characteristics of the new architecture. A new moral, a new philosophy; perhaps, in time, a new style.

ARTHUR C. HOLDEN

THE EFFECT OF FINANCE ON DESIGN

BY ARTHUR C. HOLDEN

The relation of economic factors to design possibilities, and the limitations caused by slow adjustments in this field, have already been touched on in Gordon Lorimer's paper. However, where Lorimer was concerned primarily with marketing, Holden writes of credit finance, and, in particular, long-term credit. While it may seem to some that the argument strays afield from the main subject, there can be no doubt that improvement in our physical environment depends on financing means, and that when these are less progressive than other factors in construction the result is, as Holden says, a "stultifying effect upon design."

THE true artist, who has once felt the joy of creative purpose, is thereafter moved by a natural incentive to produce. None of us will deny this. Yet the artist, irrespective of his creative urge, must learn to exchange his product for the necessities of life. Therefore the usages of exchange are important to the creative artist.

The majority of men, knowing they must live, try to direct their talents so that they can most easily assure themselves a livelihood. Shrewd men try to do those things which produce returns high in proportion to the effort expended. In this session we have discussed new construction methods and the lag in putting new methods to use, due to habits already formed.

Because of habit, a large proportion of the return for work follows accustomed channels. For example, there is a customary profit to be derived from cutting up land and selling it in lots. There is also a customary profit from the sale of building materials. This involves a complex series of profits to the original producer, profits for transportation, profits to the jobber, and frequently a commission also to the specialist who installs the material. We are accustomed also to pay a profit in the form of interest and sometimes a premium, too, for the use of money. Construction is likely to be active if profits can be made on the sale of lots, the sale of materials, and on the sale of the finished construction project.

The flow of profits into habitual channels and the dependence upon profit incentives established by habit tends to stultify innovation, creative work, and design. I mean by this design in the large sense; design as the exercise of the judgment required to make the most out of natural advantages and so to mould improvements that, at one time, they are adapted to environment, function, and so far as man can predict, to long-term need and the amenities of living. Creative design has been hampered because the designing professions have neglected to appreciate that their value to society must be expressed in terms of exchange and finance in order that the judgments and services of designers may carry weight.

Society has not yet evolved a system of long-term banking that can be compared to the achievements in short-term finance that have been developed by the commercial banks. Under the Federal Reserve System, the commercial banks may expand and contract their assets on the basis of reserves which are established on the basis of experience. In the long-term field, investment institutions and individual investors ostensibly follow a practice of making outright loans of principal. The long-term lenders, fiduciaries and others, have not yet been united into a capital reserve system with centralized reserves as a base upon which it ought to be possible to expand long-term credits in a manner similar to that employed for the expansion of short-term credits.

The way has been prepared for the next step by the firm establishment of the principle of amortization, which puts long-term credit on a returnable basis. If long-term lending agencies held to a ratio of four between expansion and reserves, they would receive as much income from 1 percent interest as they would from a rate of 4 percent paid on outright lending. An organized capital reserve system with strict requirements for amortization should make this possible.

While it is appropriate to comment upon the backwardness of long-term finance and its stultifying effect upon design, this is not the place to discuss the details of a coordinated system of capital improvement finance.

LIMITATIONS OF DISTRIBUTION

BY WALTER BAERMANN

German born, educated at the University of Munich, Baermann is an industrial designer who has divided his time between practice (independently, and with the organizations of Joseph Urban, Norman Bel Geddes, Henry Dreyfuss, Howe and Lescaze, and others) and teaching. Between 1932 and 1937 he was education director of the Springfield, Massachusetts, Museum of Fine Arts, and after that for a time consultant to the Boston and Worcester, Massachusetts, Art Museums. At one time he was head of the Industrial Design Department at Cranbrook Academy, and in 1937 he founded the California Graduate School of Design at Pasadena and remained Chairman of Faculty until 1946. At present he is in business for himself.

Mr. Baermann's thesis is that there is nothing wrong with popular taste ("public taste basically is good") and that there are plenty of capable designers, but the present "nostalgia and sentimentality" evident in the objects which add up to form our physical environment is due to advertising and other media used by those who distribute and sell designed objects. Baermann, however, is optimistic. He sees relief "on the distant horizon," to be reached principally by an improved educational system which will train man to be more selective in his purchase of the objects he needs to complete his environment. While Baermann writes as a designer of smaller objects, his argument is equally applicable to the production of buildings and communities.

IT MUST be recognized as a basic fact when we speak of those objects with which we surround ourselves that our time is equipped for mass production. We must be aware that mass production demands standardization, high speed, and production quantity greater than certain basic minimum figures. Thirdly, it must be recognized that a public nostalgia exists which, through its "style and form" sentimentality, is in direct conflict with mass production and that the distribution of those objects with which we surround ourselves exploits to the highest degree this nostalgia and sentimentality.

Retail organizations are bound to take the way of least resistance to the pocketbook of the consumer and in the majority are convinced that fostering sentimentality and associative appeals will help them in this effort. Our system of advertising is the motive power behind this attitude. Advertising has created what might be called a suggestive picture-word language which exerts an enormous impact on the millions of people. This impact not only prevents really clean technological progress, as it is based on artificial obsolescence, but also distorts and destroys basic human and social values. It even affects the sincere designer, who is eternally subject to pressures forcing him to be novel, to "streamline," to be a superficial stylist.

Since we must take the point of view that public taste basically is good, we must believe that fundamentally people want a clean, clear, comfortable, and happy surrounding. We must recognize that false decorative effects, meaningless form, hidden and unexpressed purposes, and imitation breed a false sense of possession and an utterly distorted sense of culture. The economic cycle through which products reach the consumer today has to a very high degree destroyed in him a real sense of qualitative selectiveness and has spread a superficial dollar-value consciousness.

All these negative factors cannot be remedied by designers alone. They cannot be remedied to any appreciable degree even with the cooperation of farsighted and well-meaning manufacturers. The two combined may make a dent, but the major responsibility, in my opinion, lies with the retailers, and specifically with the store buyers. Above all, the responsibility to remedy these faults lies with our educational system, which must begin to help people understand the time they live in, to understand its deeper meaning, and to build in them a selective capacity that will refuse and defy advertising slogans and empty and sentimental formalism in product development.

On the positive side of the ledger is the fact that technological ingenuity has reached the point where, in a balanced and quieted-down economy, most products can be produced at costs that will permit the great majority of people to build adequate frames for their lives. Thus, the majority of people could have an environment that would not only satisfy them but benefit them socially, intellectually, and emotionally. We believe that we can see signs on the distant horizon that a clear evaluation of these problems is beginning to take hold.

ADMINISTRATIVE LIMITATIONS

BY THEODORE T. MC CROSKY

It is appropriate at this point to have a statement from a planner who is concerned primarily with the larger design areas of replanning and rebuilding "technologically obsolete cities." The limitations facing the designer of an individual building are multiplied many times when the legal, financial, and other handicaps that stand in the way of large-scale planning are encountered, but the possibilities for an improved environment are proportionately greater if the difficulties can be overcome.

Mr. McCrosky is Director of the Greater Boston Development Committee, Inc., and before that assignment he had spent much time working in an official capacity on the planned development of Chicago and other cities.

THE theory and accepted principles of city planning and design have progressed further than the administrative and financial frameworks necessary to carry out plans. Opportunities for *de novo* city building are rare and small in scope. The most urgent problem of our age is a practical rather than a theoretical exercise: the replanning and re-building of existing but technologically obsolete cities.

The designer is faced with the task of making adequate plans that are capable of being effectuated with the public and private funds available and within the framework of constitutional law. Construction must be piecemeal, be-cause the city must maintain "business as usual." To obtain necessary funds and secure needed legislative authority, the public—the great majority of all the people—must be convinced of the importance, urgency, and desirability of planned rebuilding. The history of planning during the twentieth century bears out the belief that plans have not been realized for lack of organized public understanding and support.

A great deterrent to large-scale rebuilding operations has been and is the high price of land. Land assembly can now be achieved, under many urban redevelopment laws by eminent domain, but the obstacle of price has not yet been surmounted. The crux of the problem is that cen-trally located but blighted land commands a much higher price than its economic reuse value.

Before the professional planner and the architect can re-design and rebuild the old heart areas of our cities, these underlying and most fundamental questions of finance and law and popular support must first be answered. They have been answered in the case of many bombed-out cities in England and Europe, and there the designer is now free to go ahead. In this country, we have much inertia to over-come before we can settle the details of rebuilding plans.

The architect, engineer, or planner who engages in the solution of urban problems needs to possess not only tech-nical competence, but also large measures of imagination, practicality, and tenacity.

WHO DECIDES
WHAT IS TO BE BUILT

BY ARTHUR C. HOLDEN

There were many topics which could have consumed the entire time of the Princeton Conference by themselves. Some of those subjects were so obviously broad in scope that they were avoided by the participants in favor of more specific discussion of matters on the agenda. One such question has to do with how the decisions which control construction are made; who makes them, and for what reasons. The challenge to expand this matter was put to Arthur Holden some months after the Conference, when he was invited to address the 1947 meeting of the New York State Association of Architects on the topic which is used as the title of the following paper, which is a brief résumé of what he said at that time. The evaluation of public acceptance, the constitution of the building industry, the place of public agencies, and the need for coordination, seems very apt at this point in the discussion of limitations and possibilities.

THERE is every evidence that the public are keenly interested in knowing how they can enjoy a well-planned environment. The public, irked by prevailing inconvenience, are puzzled as to why those who purportedly understand design seem to have so little to say about the shaping of man's physical environment. Following the Conference at Princeton this question was repeatedly put to the Chairman.

Public acceptance is, of course, the final arbiter which determines the products that are offered in any market. The creation of man's physical environment is not, however, the end product of a definitely organized group of men. The great building industry which plays the largest part in shaping man's environment is a loosely organized group of highly specialized crafts and diverse types of managerial enterprise. Practically all of the demands that are made upon the building industry are for the satisfaction of particular immediate needs. The demand may be for a house for one family to live in; or for living accommodations for a number of families; or for factory space; or for a school building; or for a highway or a paved street; or for a sewer to drain a particular neighborhood. It does not always seem practical to delay decisions respecting the satisfaction of certain special immediate needs until their relation to other needs can be studied.

We know that the decisions to build are, nevertheless, the result of balancing a series of decisions. The owner's or user's decisions depend upon a host of other decisions made by the designer; by the builder; by labor; by those who supply materials; by finance; by those who control real estate; by the municipality; and by the state. It is true that as designers and coordinators, architects have a real opportunity for leadership, but where do their responsibilities begin and end?

The problems which beset our cities are the result of man's inability to foresee change and to provide for the flexibility which is the prerequisite to healthy growth. In the urgency of meeting an immediate need, the relationship to other things of what is done seldom receives adequate consideration. Buildings must be accessible and must be located on land which will be under the control of the user. The responsibility for maintaining access has been made the responsibility of local government. The responsibility of the user of a building has usually been assumed to terminate at the boundaries of his property, provided he conforms to such usages as are set by law and, through taxes, pays his share of the cost of public maintenance. Nevertheless, the way in which the boundaries of properties are laid out, as well as the way in which private properties are used, affects both the burdens that are transferred to local government and range of uses that are likely to be made of other privately owned properties.

It is true that through mapping and zoning, local government may exercise a theoretical control over access, layout, and use; but usually acts arising through private contract limit the range of governmental decisions. For example, it is easiest for a surveyor to draw rectangular grids setting the boundaries between private properties, but such a pattern of property boundaries may make it difficult to work out an economic or efficient pattern of public streets. Some cities have tried to protect themselves against the difficulties of inadequate streets by requiring that all streets provide for average expected traffic. There is, however, no such thing as average traffic, and it is impossible to determine the demands of either moving traffic or parking, until the relationships of land use have begun to become evident. Changes in uses of private property generate changes in traffic flow and require changes in public planning. It is apparent that a greater degree of coordination is required between public administration and the administration of privately owned real properties.

Due to the great increase in the size of our cities, the individual property owner has been losing touch with those responsible for the policies of city government, and, worse yet, those responsible for municipal administration have been losing contact with the needs, the problems, and the plight of the small property owner. Little villages have been swallowed up in great cities. Small groups of neighbors no longer have an agency through which they can act. To reinvigorate the life in localities we need to redevelop a means of local self-expression.

In 1941 the State of New York passed its first urban redevelopment act. This aimed to give the majority of the property owners in a blighted district the power to replan and redevelop their properties. (Long ago, before the feudal system was clamped upon Europe, periodic redistributions of agricultural properties had been an accepted practice.) There did not appear to be, however, any recent constitutional precedent for pooling properties with a trustee for the purpose of replanning and reapportionment on the basis of an equitable appraisal. Therefore, in framing the first urban redevelopment law, the power of eminent domain was invoked, on the theory that property had to be taken away from existing owners for the public purpose of replanning, and that after replanning property might be disposed of in any means permitted by law rather than reapportioned and returned to the original owners by mutual agreement.

The battle for individual rights and the struggle against landlordism, which have taken place since the abolition of the feudal system, have obscured some of the ideas about cooperation and common interests in property which were known to our ancestors. Our grandmothers have passed on to us stories about the quilting bee when neighbors, by sharing labor, turned drudgery into social relaxation. The quilting bee taught our ancestors the value of social cooperation. Our grandfathers have told us also about the barn raising parties, and the beer that was served, when the neighbors came in and helped to raise the heavy timbers that had been hewn and fitted for mortise and tenon by the owner and his helper. The barn raising was another evidence of social cooperation.

Salem, Massachusetts, was once the center of an embryonic cattle industry. It was for this reason that the freeholders of Salem originally set aside a greater proportion of common lands than any other New England city. Salem's common lands were administered by trustees for two hundred years. The administration of common lands was a recognized form of social cooperation.

The needs of our own day have tended to create special instrumentalities. We have created housing authorities, bridge authorities, and port authorities. We have created great mutual societies to administer insurance services. We have created specific types of public service corporations to furnish utility services. There are times when because of their size or their abuse of power we lose sight of the significance of these special agencies. Sometimes we fail to distinguish these types of common and cooperative services from governmental services. Nevertheless the formation of associations for the performance of special services is the democratic way of approach. It should be possible for us to make better and greater use of corporate trustees to take the responsibility for decisions which affect the basic common interests of groups of citizens. Certainly individual decisions, which must be made by owners, by construction, by finance, by the users of realty, and by the municipality, should be coordinated with decisions which take common interests into consideration.

In planning for the improvement of man's environment, we must recognize that the decision to build is not something finite and individual but the result of a series of decisions which must take place and which affect the character of building. Upon intelligence and understanding depend the possibilities for coordination and for leadership. There is no greater need in present day society than for an understanding of the part which various specialists play in the shaping of decisions. If the nineteenth century may be said to have ushered in an age of specialization, let it be hoped that it will be the achievement of the twentieth century to develop the art of coordination.

PROGRAMMING: A CREATIVE ACT

BY RICHARD J. NEUTRA

In the paper that follows, Richard Neutra discusses the *program* under which the architect-planner works as a limitation on both his design endeavors and public understanding and support of the move toward a better physical environment. If the designer were called in on the development of the program, says Neutra in effect, he would have a better understanding of what he is doing, and proper and realistic funds could be requisitioned. There is no doubt that the piecemeal approach, the inadequate financing and the insufficient legislative authority which Theodore McCrosky complained of could often be alleviated if programming were considered not a job for an unimaginative bureaucrat, but rather a "creative art" requiring "a foresight which activates, which is imaginative, and which is not bound . . . to the obvious."

Richard Neutra, born in Vienna in 1892, educated in Austria and Switzerland, came to the United States in 1923 after a practice abroad as architect and city planner. His work has had a strong influence on the development of design—some of his individual houses and housing projects have become contemporary classics—and he has written a great deal on design, planning, and construction methods. Although his practice has centered in California, where he has been Chairman of the State Planning Board and a member of the State Board of Examiners, he has ranged far afield from that state in his commissions, and as lecturer and consultant. At various times he has been retained as a consultant to the U.S. Housing Authority, the Federal Works Agency, and the Federal Public Housing Authority; from the background of experience which these positions give him, Neutra speaks with feeling as well as authority of the importance of the program.

IS THE architect-planner simply a caterer to requirements stated by others? Where over-all instituted authorities do a job of consistent wholesale programming, it is easy to confine the role of a particular designer-planner to receiving and accepting a slice of this program: it is assumed he will acquiesce and live up to the physical terms of his project. Whether the society which thus employs this professional be run, politically speaking, by a tyrant or a small clique, or whether it be collective or democratic, it may consider the designing professional who develops the habit of questioning the program as unruly and lacking in discipline.

However, at this date and in this part of the world, the programming of even large communities is still budgeted with funds so diminutive in comparison to the task that a penetrating program or a well-considered guide line that can be successfully adhered to is rather rare. The inertia which expresses itself as a desire to prevent worse conditions and police what exists is not equivalent to a program.

Rio de Janeiro has had until recently, we learn, an annual budget of $26,000 for programming or master-planning a metropolitan area of about two and one-half million people which, in its longest dimension, stretches sixty-five miles. Los Angeles, until about the beginning of the war, had to get along on a $75,000-a-year budget to program action for approximately five hundred square miles, and fit it into a vast, semi-urbanized region of accelerated multi-form development and overlapping jurisdictions. Meanwhile, a huge planning fee approaching a million dollars may be paid for the questionable design of a city hall—a simple enough task compared to the outlining of even a small part of a city.

We have not generally grasped the cost and the responsibility of programming before plotting and building. The amount of creative intuition as well as systematic work that goes into it and the effect which this early planning has on the final design solution are only vaguely, if at all, understood in proportion to their true significance.

The question, therefore, of whether the planning-designing profession shall cater to a poorly considered requirement list, handed to it by the "owner," is in need of discussion. This is conspicuously true when the professional is commissioned by a government agency where, as in the case of a housing project, his skill, training, and experience are assumed as superior to, and his compensation is set higher than, that of the organs employed to program his work. He often receives most rigid directives, preliminaries, and standards, and yet not rarely is paid a handsome if controversial fee for acting as a mere technician. Amount of compensation may not at all be the best scale by which to measure professional fitness and quality of output. But if the executing architect is to abide by a programmatic list, this probably should, for best results, be developed by a set of professionals more ingenious than himself, and properly compensated.

The major brain investment is in the program, a preliminary which is fertile with potential life only if it digests all supposedly "realistic" requirements in the light and radiation of a humane foresight which activates, which is imaginative, and which is not bound to the pedestrian statistics of the past or to the obvious. Programming is a creative art.

Every owner should be guided to see the planning professional in the light of a program consultant. It is shortsighted, under the present circumstances of disorder in planning programs, to make the architect-planner simply subservient to a set list of requirements and rules. No one else's qualifications for developing the program can be substituted for the ultimate designer's questioning of the premises under which these requirements were drawn up.

There is a physiological brain mechanism that seems automatically to link programming and design—to consider the earlier and later phases of programming an already subconsciously *anticipated* design solution and an implicit, *pre-formed* design decision. Any judge of an open competition can exercise his psychological interest in the way the contestants have obviously searched the program for "implied solutions." Perhaps, sometime in the future, this reaction will be understood; then a practical conclusion on the best possible procedure and the proper relation of program to solution will be found. The problem is of most profound importance for the outcome of the broad designing and planning activity to which mankind seems more and more officially pledged with the passage of current civilized history.

It was from this point of view that I gained a double and generic interest in the recent "two-legged" competition for a comprehensive cultural and city planning task in St. Louis, posed nationally for optimum results.* The professional adviser's concept there—to make the material premiated in the first submission of the contest a frank contribution to the program for the next step, and the winners of the first round natural co-advisers or members of a program committee since they would be *creatively oriented* and informed of the problems *through their own active efforts toward a solution*—may not, in fact, have been followed in complete detail. But it demonstrates in sharp

* The Jefferson National Expansion Memorial Competition. George Howe, Professional Adviser, wrote the program for the first stage, which was open to all designers. Five winners were chosen from this first "round" to compete for the final solution. Program for the second stage was not written until the five had been selected, and was based largely on their studies. Mr. Neutra was a member of the jury.—Ed.

illumination what I would like to call the *creative familiarity* with a task to be programmed, something which cannot be dispensed with, or substituted for, without severe loss. It is significantly distinguishable from the best tabulated anthology of facts and figures, which is often prepared so voluminously as to become a "fact-finding farce" that confines the scope of any design ability and under all its dead weight is barren, without a spark of creative stimulation.

SECTION III

FORM

INTRODUCTION

BY THOMAS H. CREIGHTON

I T IS in the realm of esthetics that an architectural discussion or symposium most often bogs down. Personal prejudices, the influence of tradition, the introduction of undefinable emotional or "spiritual" values above the purely utilitarian—one or more of these intangibles enter the field in time to render previous agreements useless as bases on which to develop a three-dimensional architectural expression. At the Princeton Conference there was agreement on the reason for architecture—the human and social need of a proper physical environment—and agreement that the physical possibilities peculiar to our time must be more fully exploited, and their limitations studied. Next the group turns its attention to the design forms which must result from such needs and such possibilities and limitations.

One of the most significant things about this particular group discussion is that it moves the consideration of form from the vague place it has had in the design of usable shelter to its proper position as a source of physical sensations which have a strong effect on men's lives. There it can be studied, scientifically. There it can be discussed on rational, rather than emotional, terms.

The Conference does not come through with ready answers. It rather prepares a position, from which further studies can be evolved. That position might be stated as follows: Esthetic values in architecture are not a physical addition (out with the early nineteenth century definition of architecture as the decoration of construction) nor an intellectual exercise (out with the early twentieth century definition of architecture as a mathematical creation of the mind) but rather they are sensory visual reactions due to education, past association, and an intuitive sense of value and use which the beholder relates to the form. What creates this sense of purposeful value—the innate favorable esthetic reaction—is best defined in the papers that follow, not by an architect, but by a psychologist, Adelbert Ames, who says, "the form of the artifact should be such as visually to disclose to those who may want to use it what it is useful for."

It was apparent from the early correspondence that the discussants were not going to be satisfied with any definition of esthetics which considered such values as something arbitrarily added to a utilitarian object. Giedion's statement that "esthetic values are inherent in things," and Holden's that he did not believe "esthetic value can be created through conscious aim. Esthetic value is the evidence of an innate harmony," were foreseen by Talbot Hamlin, who wrote before the Conference:

The experience of what we call "beauty" seems to me to be one of the prime requirements for psychological health. If the development of a rich life in the emotional sense—the stimulation of the greatest potentialities for the noble enjoyment in individual lives—is of primary importance, then the problem of esthetics in architecture becomes not at all the problem of adding a necessary luxury to a design the primary purpose of which is to be hygienic and utilitarian; it is rather an essential part of the contribution architecture can make to human life.

Professor Ames replied to Hamlin, agreeing, but translating the statement into terms of his own research. At Dartmouth since 1919, and now at the Hanover Institute, Ames and his associates have been studying vision, visual sensations, and increasingly the relation of vision to human behavior. While the Institute states clearly in its published literature that "a complete understanding of these findings can be given only by lengthy exposition and the personal experiencing of numerous phenomena through laboratory demonstrations,"* and Professor Ames was at first reluctant

* Certain of the Dartmouth Eye Institute laboratory apparatus was set up at Princeton, and participants in the Conference were guided through the experiments.

to translate his findings into architectural terms, he finally did. If it is possible in a few words to summarize the work of the Dartmouth group, it can probably best be done in their own words:

Our disclosures apparently show . . . that the objective significances to which we react do not exist in externality in their own right but are our own personal creations. That is, the human organism *acts* because of physiological stimuli; but contrary to traditional and wholly gratuitous assumption, *these stimuli have in themselves no meaning to the organism.* The significances that are related to stimuli *in consciousness* and that are experienced by the organism as sensations *are its own creation, derived entirely from the organism's individual experience and inherited characteristics.* The function of sensations (perceptions) is not to disclose objective characteristics of externality as such. They are prognostive directives for purposeful action.

Without being previously familiar with the Dartmouth findings, a number of the participants in early correspondence found their thinking on esthetics tending in the direction of the physiological and psychological aspects of visual sensations. For example, Gordon Lorimer wrote of his belief that "the difficulty in achieving visual harmony in a freshly creative manner lies in the habit of the eye. Like new music, new architectural forms may appear strange and forbidding, yet with greater familiarity grow intensely satisfying." In a similar vein another participant wrote that he believed "the philosophic and psychological consideration of form is a study of human reactions. The esthetic experience is a personal one . . . formistic associations are at once the most annoying and the most persistent of the forces acting on the arrangement of form." Henry Churchill replied that he agreed that the matter of "formistic associations" touched off "a whole field of speculation." He referred to the work of the Hanover Institute, and said he felt it "seems to be a first step towards a scientific analysis of esthetics."

So Professor Ames agreed to join the discussion, and he replied, before the meeting itself, to Talbot Hamlin's remark on "the experience of what we call beauty" by saying that he would translate it into his own words, as follows:

To fulfill its function all architecture must be designed so that beyond meeting the necessary functional uses its form should be such as to give rise in the beholder to value-sense experiences (esthetic experiences).

The matter of *personal* reactions to esthetic experiences receives a good deal of consideration. If the reaction is a purely individual one, then many schools of criticism are wrong: the value to any one person of his own esthetic reactions must be judged in relation to his own course of action, his own behavior, his own life. Talbot Hamlin, carrying to this sphere his argument in the previous section against standardization, had this to say:

The world is full of all kinds of people. People who like the country and people who like crowds, large families and small, old people and young people, people who like to be close to the earth and love to putter in gardens, and people to whom contact with the earth means only sunburn and lame backs. There are people who like the sense of openness and people who like the sense of privacy. Now as I see it there is nothing fundamentally wrong or anti-social in being one sort of person or another. In fact, I should say further that the richness of a community life will frequently be conditioned by the variety of the temperaments of its members.

Considering this argument from the point of view of his researches, Ames replied that since "every individual is confronted by the personal responsibility of carrying out his purposes, urges, and drives" in his own unique manner, he agreed with Hamlin's thesis. While he felt that "the form of buildings used in common by the public should be such as to arouse visual awareness of potential purposes and value satisfactions common to the whole group," he wrote to Hamlin, as he states in his final paper, that he felt individual homes should be individually designed for their owners. He stated it thus:

All private homes should be designed (as far as possible) to enable the owner to carry out his unique purposes and interests and also so that he may experience his unique value-sense experience.

The "as far as possible" is undoubtedly a bow to the limitations which bring about the need for standardized low-cost individual homes and living quarters for rent, which obviously cannot be designed to satisfy any one individual family's "value-sense."

This point of view, with the elaboration of it in several of the papers that follow, raises this particular architectural discussion above the level of those in the past that have reduced esthetics to a matter of "styles." The closest approach to the eclectic manner of thinking is in Professor Theodore M. Greene's paper. After agreeing with Ames's thesis (in philosopher's rather than psychologist's words) by stating his belief that design can achieve a form which is "expressive of the emotions, feelings, and moods characteristic of the human activities which the building houses," he goes on to say that this expression should be "in the language of an appropriate style." For the rest, stylism, either modern or traditional, did not enter the discussion in this section. (In the later discussion in Section VI the question did come up again briefly.)

In some of the pre-Conference exchange of opinions, there was apparent a desire to avoid reducing the discussion to the worn-out modernist vs. traditionalist battle. Some discussants appeared anxious to avoid falling into the trap of speaking of a "modern style"; others wished there could be a rational definition of "tradition." Walter Gropius asked if the discussants could not "undertake to find a definition of what tradition is." He added the beautiful understatement that "it would be a great help." In his usual caustic vein, George Howe advised that it might be better to avoid the use of the word. He said:

You speak of defining tradition. I think the idea cannot

be too often considered, but the word should be avoided. Traditionalist has become, by connotation, a fighting name. In 1931, speaking before the annual meeting of the AIA, I discussed the meaning of tradition in action at some, perhaps too great, length. I began, if I remember rightly, by saying that tradition should be a burr in the seat of the understanding instead of, as traditionalists would have it, the name of a mattress particularly conducive to sleep—"Beauty Rest."

The Conference seems to have established the theses, then, that esthetic value should be inherent in an architectural form, not added to it, and that the esthetic reaction of the beholder will depend largely on the apparent value of the form to him. No stronger argument for an "organic" architecture has ever been stated, nor has a better case ever been made for a study of esthetics as the essential, basic appropriateness of the form of an architectural object. And yet there persists the fact, known to all practicing architects and substantiated by Ames's findings, that the "purposeful value" of a structure is indicated, visually, largely through education and past association. There is the paradox that an individual brought up to associate a completely inappropriate form with, for example, a church structure, will be emotionally satisfied each time he visually associates that form with that use. Yet, as Ames points out, this is an unsatisfactory situation, psychologically. If the qualities suggested by "pure form" are incongruous with the true purposes, then "it would be worse than if no value-quality were suggested at all." Emerging, as we are, from an eclectic period when the "purposeful value" of a structure has been expressed by the choice of "an appropriate style," this problem is a particularly knotty one.

One answer, to which psychologists, philosophers, architects, and engineers seem agreed in principle if not in practice, is that a logical "readable" use of *structural* forms is the surest base on which to build a principle of esthetics. The many vague generalities that have been written about the need for design "expressing" structure begin to make esthetic sense when honestly apparent structure is considered one of the "indications or clues" that must build up and supplement one another to produce what Ames calls the "sense of surety" in the beholder. Walter Taylor posed this attitude, as a question, in pre-Conference correspondence:

Historically the structural mode has been the principal character-giving factor in the art of architecture. The vapid character of much of the Renaissance and the confusion of nineteenth century eclecticism may be traced to a lack of sense of structural principle as basic in design. The structural forms used were used imitatively, vicariously, or symbolically.

Much of contemporary non-traditional design is ineffectual and unconvincing because the designers, lacking a true understanding of structural principles, have assembled meaningless groupings of twentieth century structural members, using them falsely and vicariously as the Renaissance used classic structural forms.

What of esthetic design in terms of the present highly complex assemblies determined by structural engineering design—continuous slabs and beams, including cantilevers, bird cage skeleton, parabolic reinforced concrete and laminated arches and vaults, skin-stressed panels, etc.?

The untrained layman can easily grasp the simple gravitational principles in the post and lintel, and even the dynamics of an arch. Does the layman have a secondary instinct, a subconscious sense of structure, of the same order as his sense of gravity and balance? Is he capable of feeling a mathematical and physical "rightness" of structural form? In other words, is architectural esthetic only optical and formal?

Even though speaking of the appropriate use of structural systems, Taylor worries about "the untrained layman." This matter of the untrained, or poorly "trained" general public (the man and the society for whom architecture is devised) comes back again to past associations and leads inevitably to a consideration of general education. As Arthur Holden expresses it, "Unfortunately the inexperienced mind has not seen enough of good design to be sensitive to disharmony." Sigfried Giedion, pointing to the lack of official "acceptance" of Robert Maillart's bridge design in Switzerland, leads through his entire paper to an appeal for improved educational methods. His remark that "we have to prepare the next generation for these enormous tasks lying ahead" would have seemed out of place in a discussion of esthetics, had not the ground been laid by Ames in his statement that "sensations are only prognostive directives for potential action."

There is no smug intra-professional conclusion in these papers that architectural design is the business of the architect, and that the public must be educated to "appreciate" the architect. There is throughout an indicated sense of responsibility; a responsibility to *better* man's physical environment, not only through the utility of the structures designed, but equally through the forms chosen for their design, and the impact of those forms on the society in which man lives.

It would not be fair to say that in the papers presented here or in the discussion between sessions at Princeton there was a complete absence of yearning for enrichment of the basic useful form. While repudiating the solution based on arbitrarily applied ornament, the discussants reached for a better one. Greene says that it is the architect's responsibility to lead the way "toward the eradication of human frustration *and the enrichment* of human life" (my italics). Hudnut is sure that "we have not forgotten that the art of building is, like painting and music, a fine art." Walker comes to the rather debatable conclusion that the distinction between "aristocratic and proletarian concepts of leadership in space use" is what makes the difference between the simply useful and the beautifully useful. "Pueblo man," he says, "achieves the hut. . . . The aristocrat aspires to the cathedral."

With this *reductio ad absurdum* the answer perhaps finds

itself. Arthur E. Morgan, in a letter before the Conference to Arthur Holden, provided in advance one reply to Walker's thesis. He wrote:

Men or institutions that have fully arrived do not worry about prestige. It is men and institutions that lack a feeling of security which try to compensate for that lack by ostentation. I have often wished that American democracy could take itself for granted in its architecture and not constantly announce to the world, "See, we are big and strong and wealthy. We can afford imposing expenditure." I incline to the opinion that really great architecture would be relatively modest in its expression, and that we never shall achieve great architecture until we can overcome our sense of insecurity and inferiority, with the resulting craving for power.

No, it is not that the aristocrat wants "esthetic pleasure" and the ordinary man does not. As Giedion says, "If man's emotional needs are not satisfied, he will react immediately." So we come back to the "ancient criteria" that Hudnut refers to—proportion, rhythmic relationship, harmonies in texture and color. Nothing in the psychological or physiological or philosophical attitude that dominates the discussion denies this. In fact, one other ancient criterion assumes greater importance than ever. That is the matter of scale—and in this context, *human* scale. Walter Gropius wrote of this before the Conference in words which supplement Morgan's comments above:

... The Roman Caesars with their megalomania spoiled western architecture until now by huge axes and overgrown distances from building to building. Now once more the simple human being and not the Caesars is what matters, so we have to study his way of life, his manner of seeing, his experience of distance, in order to grasp what scale will fit him.

And, as Professor Greene expresses it more philosophically, there is the responsibility to study "scale as an architectural expression of the human spirit."

CONCEPTS OF SPACE AND FORM

BY RALPH WALKER

Member of the New York architectural firm of Voorhees, Walker, Foley & Smith, Ralph Walker is a Fellow in the American Institute of Architects, has been an active practitioner since his education at M.I.T., and is an ardent discussant of architectural theory.

Walker's concepts are always peculiarly his own. Much of the attitude toward South American modern architecture which appears in his paper developed during a recent trip he made to that part of America as an AIA delegate to the 1947 Inter-American conference on architecture in Lima, Peru. The middle section of his paper, dealing with a fear that the machine and its result—standardization—may become man's master, may be compared with the more technical discussion of this subject in the preceding section. Walker's philosophical interest in the effect of machine technologies on architectural form belongs more fairly here than in the previous subject matter, which was possibilities and limitations. Mr. Walker's paper is presented first, since he was chairman of this part of the discussion at Princeton.

IT IS obvious that man occupies space which has always existed: that when man builds he merely molds that space to meet his immediate needs. These needs are greatly varied from a simple shelter (which can be achieved by hides, mud, thatch, or beaten-out oil tins) to achievements of great symbolism. Therefore, the use to which space is molded gives it its human determinations—its concept of a society.

A pragmatic people such as the ancient Spartan Commune achieved qualities of space quite different from that finally arrived at under the Roman Empire. A Quaker Meeting House presents a different fundamental philosophy than does a Roman Catholic Church. (Here the plainness of one has no greater moral value than the richness of the other.) It will be obvious that different proportions will arise from a religious philosophy where the priest makes his prayers standing erect and one where the priest officiates when supine. A hospitable people will want in the simplest shelter that symbolic quality which will not be found among the parsimonious. And finally a free people will desire another quality than that permitted in a police state. A communist will have difficulty in achieving a religious atmosphere—Niemeyer's little chapel near Belo Horizonte in Brasil is an outstanding example of such a failure. The world-wide influence of Corbusier is one of a philosophy.

The mastery of space can be found only in its human use. Proportions are given additional value by aristocratic or proletarian concepts of leadership in space use. We find one concept in the pueblos of New Mexico. Here no aristocracy has ever arisen—the whole character of the community follows the leadership ideals found within it. Contrast this form of space with that evolved in Salem, Massachusetts, in the years just previous to 1812; the latter developed fine proportions in every level of the community, achieving them by freeing the ideals of leadership and offering widening opportunities. The pueblo looks ever inward upon itself—the clipper-building seaport looked ever outward to the larger world. One society is proletarian, desiring above all security within its mass; the other aristocratic and, in the best sense, adventurous. While it may be true that no modern society can disregard the common man, it will fail unless it also offers the opportunities of leadership to some higher building idea than mere shelter.

Most modern housing projects the world over are pueblo proportioned and pueblo secured. One expects to find a keener and wider, a nobler sense of space use esthetics in a community given to an adventurous life. Pueblo man readily achieves the hut, the mean, the barely adequate. The aristocrat aspires to the cathedral, noble heights.

Other than in space and proportion there is esthetic pleasure in the degree of perfection attainable or desired. Tools and methods are extensions of man's desire to create. He has made of his own hands one of the supreme tools he has ever conceived—without them no other tool or process could possibly have arrived. These hands are man's supreme invention, capable of the utmost delicacy and precision. Tools and methods are extensions of the power of man's hands—a machine, crude or electronic, is a creature of man's will to create. In primitive societies where the external tool is new in remembrance and the results personally gratifying, it is apt to develop a quality of animism —in other words, "Der is no hammer like mah hammer." This tends to limit the enlarging abilities inherent in the creative mind and in the development of new power extensions.

Today there has developed the idea that the machine in itself determines the characteristics of the product—that because the machine does *easily* certain operations in repetition, the product must conform to these limited operations. The machine must, however, do more than stamp, crimp, roll, punch, to meet the enlarging human necessity. The first use of the potter's wheel must have shaken the "coil makers" of pottery and it must have been generally agreed that it would limit the shapes of things—"they must all be 'round.' " The history of porcelain denies any such limitation.

A friend of mine has a nasty lighting fixture in his office, two of them in fact, two complete globes hanging in space like two suns. They came out of the Bauhaus concept of mechanical design but contain no basis of scientific knowledge of lighting—of man's physiology. Still they persist although lighting engineer, ophthalmologist, humanist, deny them any virtue: *but* the "machine limiter" thinks that inasmuch as they are simple in form, they are necessarily desirable. Here is an animism of idea that there is virtue in a standard scientifically thought bad. The eyes and the body endure fatigue because there has been a limitation to what the "tool" may accomplish.* This is the fault in much modern design which places an "appearance"

* See page 26, *Walter Gropius, The New Architecture and the Bauhaus,* Museum of Modern Art, 1936. See also "Good Lighting for People at Work in Reading Rooms and Offices," Division of Research, Graduate School of Business Administration, Harvard University.—R.W.

of machine simplicity above the research knowledge of the time, much of which is especially able in relation to human physiology.

This animistic approach to the tool proclaims the desirability of complete standardization which will mean that invention comes too quickly to a standstill, a condition contrary to the idea of the machine world itself. Aldous Huxley expresses this philosophy in *Brave New World*— "Never mend, always spend"—an assembly line goes on but always with a new model just around the corner. If this were not so, perhaps those who prefer the products of the eighteenth century are right.*

The only complete standardization will be found in heaven and even there one is not sure that the Almighty, as in "Green Pastures," is not time and time again changing His concept of His own knowledge. The modern world is driven on to this destroying standardization which can only mean enslavement to the machine itself. Freedom means an understanding of human physiology and psychology. What you like and what I like may be instructive in relation to design—but instructive because we appreciate the fact that it is influenced largely by our own traditions. The Average likes a free-burning fire in a fireplace indoors or out. One may never add up all that this fireplace means to mankind in its symbols of comfort, of home, family, endurance. Added to this, however, is the contrary force of words. We must be modern—an oil burner is more efficient in fact. What hold has sentiment in the search for efficiency?

* "New how-to-do's (i.e., methods of production, communication, warfare, etc.) produce new ways of thinking which become standardized for a time as norms but which in turn become obsolete as other how-to-do's are discovered and invented by man. In connection with new how-to-do's, new norms evolve and they, in turn, become obsolete." *Understanding Man's Social Behavior: Preliminary Notes.* Hadley Cantril. Office of Public Opinion Research, Princeton, N.J., 1947. p. 15. Professor Cantril, who was an observer at the Conference where these papers were read, has made important applications of the research which Adelbert Ames, Jr., reports on in the next paper.—Ed.

The modern historian tries to write the history of future endeavors—as a commentator he often tries to act as a creator. The critic judges the surface, makes a phrase and either damns or praises a result. We discover the historian and the philosopher alike acting as interpreters long before the evidence is all in. The power of propaganda influences the judgment of the historian. The photograph, which rarely tells a story completely or with accuracy, influences people who have not had the opportunity of judging the actual result. In Lima, Peru, where an umbrella cloud hides the city for six months of the year, an architect copies the *brise soleil*. The dramatic physical takes the place of the dramatic human. The "four-leaf clover" against the family place of peace, individual enlargement, and spiritual adventures. "Plasticity" versus serenity, which is quite different from leading the vegetable life of the permanent proletariat.

There is land enough all over the world to take care comfortably of greatly increased populations. When you hear that the land in England is limited, it means that it is limited under a present economy—under one idea. Nowhere, however, does Corbusier's idea of the skyscraper high on "pilotis" mean that the land is better used for human use. "The large building groups stand on pillars so that the ground is unobstructed for the pedestrian. The open space rescued by this concentration in height and in great units is used for landscaping, nurseries, cinemas, sports. Even the twelve percent of the ground covered by the building is available for recreation, for the flat roofs are transformed into playgrounds and solaria."* At no time has Corbusier, whose ideas are incorporated in the sentence just quoted, ever asked whether people prefer to live in the slab buildings proposed by the members of the CIAM. And all over the world so powerful is the influence of word and photograph propaganda, architects are trying to make people live in these tall slabs. (Recently the Planning and Housing di-

* *Space, Time and Architecture*, Sigfried Giedion, 1941.

rectors of Santiago de Chile, the Planning Director of Buenos Aires, and the Planning Director of Rio stated that the vast majority of the people of each of these cities preferred to have single family houses with patios of their own. Nevertheless, in Rio, adjoining the most unoccupied land in the world, the "Ciudad dos Motores" is contemplated—more and more "slabs"—wholly in contrast to the desires of the people as to the way they would like to be housed—wholly because of the influence of the printed word on architects who insist on a new esthetic which does not have any real economy in the basis of its idea. Our own Gallup polls add up to the same story of single family houses.)

The artist no longer in tune with the people of his community—dissociated from the emotions common to high and low alike—is forced to admit he no longer touches the great group of people and is quite content to claim, "I am misunderstood," and moreover to look at anyone who claims that the artist is understood with amused skepticism. Picasso says Gertrude Stein did not understand him. It is generally acknowledged that if you do not admire an artist by observation or emotional appeal, you are ignorant of his intellectual intent—perhaps if you read about him you may understand what others believe he represents. So you have more works about a man than you have his works of accomplishment. The "phrase maker" has used the machine, i.e., the printing press, to gain an unusual and strangely powerful influence. So the pen is mightier than the brush.

Me! I desire a much more simple society in which the family, the community, and the artisan understand each other and whose teamwork is wholly voluntary and not externally imposed.

ARCHITECTURAL FORM AND VISUAL SENSATIONS

BY ADELBERT AMES, JR.

As Research Professor in psychological optics at Dartmouth, Ames has carried on a series of studies at the Dartmouth Eye Institute from 1919 until last year. The work is now being continued at the Hanover Institute. Increasingly, experts in the various disciplines have become interested in the implications of his studies in visual sensations, their nature and their effect on man and on society. As stated earlier, Ames was at first reluctant to attempt an application to the field of architecture. He has said, "Our experience in the field is too meager to provide a background necessary for wisdom."

The psychological data is there for architects to make use of. Not all of them will like its implications. When an attempt was made recently to present to an architectural audience what Ames kindly called a "concise and communicable statement" on the studies,* several readers cried out in anguish that this seemed to outlaw any "element of surprise or shock," or "purgative or cathartic" intention for architecture. It does indeed. In addition, the careful reader will notice a number of points in which Ames' paper differs from Walker's in more than the choice of words from the psychologist's vocabulary.

I HAVE been asked to speak to you on the significance of the disclosures of our research in vision to the problem of planning man's physical environment, especially in regard to the philosophy of form and the psychological effect of form. It would seem that the significance may be quite profound. But I am appalled by the difficulty of making clear to you why that may be so.

Our research in the origin and nature of perception shows that vision is quite a different phenomenon from what most of us believe. Further, an understanding of vision, more specifically of the origin and nature of our visual sensations, apparently shows that man's relationship to his physical environment and therefore to his artifacts is also quite different from what most of us believe.

* *Progressive Architecture*, December, 1947. p. 20.

We commonly believe that man's physical environment is something unrelated to man, existing apart from man, in its own right.

While in no way denying the existence of the "external world," our disclosures apparently show that the only aspects of it that man can know anything about are those aspects that are either helpful or thwarting in carrying out his purposes.

Our disclosures apparently show:

1. That the qualities and characteristics that constitute the visual sensations of which we are conscious when we have a visual experience are not inherent in the so-called external "things" at which we are looking.

2. We would not have sensations *but for* external events, *but for* the light rays that impinge upon us and *but for* our physiological stimulus patterns resulting from those impingements. However, (a) the origin of our sensations is in our prior experiences and (b) the characteristics and qualities of our sensations are determined by our particular unique personal history.

3. Our sensations are not absolute disclosures to us of inherent characteristics of external events ("things"). They only disclose the significances that external events ("things") may have to us as particular unique human beings.

4. Sensations are only prognostic directives for potential action in the furtherance of our valueful purposes, which are recognized by us partially in the form of logical concepts but to a greater degree by an "intuitive" awareness of value-quality.

5. Our sensations do not come into being as completed wholes but are most complicated integrations of innumerable indications or clues.

6. These indications or clues may supplement each other or they may be in varying degrees of conflict.

7. To the degree that these indications and clues supplement each other we have a "sense of surety" in the prognostic reliability of our sensations. To the degree that they

do not supplement each other we have a corresponding "sense of lack of surety."

8. Our purposes range from passing, trivial wishes through deep-seated desire for security to insistence for continual improvement of our lot, i.e., for directional evolving emergence to higher and higher levels of being. And at the present period in the evolution of the human race this emergence is particularly rapid.*

If the above disclosures are applied to our understanding of a concrete experiential situation, the results, stated in most general terms, would be something like this. Suppose we look at something, say a chair. The elements that go to make up the total visual sensations of which we are conscious, such as size, shape, tridimensionality, distance, chairness, resting, relaxing, comfort, etc., etc., do not exist inherently in the "thing" we are looking at, but in fact have their origin entirely in our past experiences. Our sensations are our personal creations, a synthesis of significances to us that we have learned from prior experiences with similar "things" involving not only the practical uses of which we are conceptually aware, but also, and more important, the innumerable intuitively sensed value-qualities related to value-satisfactions that we were aware of during those prior experiences.†

To understand how the above-mentioned disclosures are related to the problems of architecture, the following facts must be borne in mind: Every individual is confronted by the personal responsibility of carrying out his purposes, urges, and drives which he inherited in his unique chromosome pattern and which are characteristically unique to

* Compare this analysis with Ralph Walker's description in the preceding paper of the "permanent proletariat" who desires security, but aspires only to the hut.—Ed.

† For a more complete grasp of the bearing of these disclosures on our understanding of perception refer to *Understanding Man's Social Behavior* by Professor Hadley Cantril of Princeton (Office of Public Opinion Research, Princeton, N.J.) and *Education for What is Real*, by Earl C. Kelley (Harper & Bros., New York, 1947).—A.A.Jr.

him, and different from those of every other individual.

He has to carry out his unique purposes, urges, and drives in an externality, so to speak, which is different from any externality that ever existed before and is different from the externality by which any other individual is confronted. This is true both for the reason that "nature never repeats itself" and also for the reason that each individual plays a role in creating his particular externality.

In carrying out his purposes, urges, and drives, the efforts of every person will meet with interference of three different types: (1) He will be blocked by inanimate nature and the indeterminable emergent changes in inanimate nature. (2) He will be blocked by the action of other persons who, like himself, are carrying out their unique individual purposes, unless their purposes are identical to his own. (3) He will be blocked by group mores and customs.

When a person is blocked in his attempts to carry out his purposes, he is frustrated. He can solve his frustration only by altering his so-called "externality" and/or by altering his drives or purposes.

Man is unique among organisms in his ability to alter externality and is greatly facilitated in carrying out his purposes by his capacity to create artifacts, ranging from the stone hatchet of the far past to the atom bomb of the present.

It follows that planning man's physical environment involves taking stock of what can be done to modify and affect externality most effectively so that man can more successfully carry out his purposes in the direction of their evolutionary emergence.

Architecture is an example of the highest type of artifact that man has devised to help him carry out his purposes. Architects are the high priests and are responsible for the effective construction and evolution of this most important type of artifact. In connection with that responsibility what we have said emphasizes and confirms the generally accepted "functional" hypothesis that buildings are but sticks and stones except insofar as they serve man in carrying out his purposes. For if the only reason man creates artifacts is to help him carry out his purposes, it of necessity follows that the form of the artifact should be such that those who look at it will be unequivocally aware of what it is used for. That is, a hammer should look like something to drive nails with and not like a monkey wrench, which is used to turn nuts.

We can know that an artifact "looks like something" not because of what it may actually be able to be used for but only because of our prior experience. For example, a person can know that a certain artifact looks like a hammer only because of his prior experience with artifacts of similar form which he knows drive nails. Put a pneumatic hammer before him, and if he had had no prior experience with it, he wouldn't know it was a hammer.

This means that in his use of form an architect must take into account the prior experience of the people who are going to look at his artifacts.

Where he has the opportunity through the development of new materials to improve the use of an artifact, he should retain the old form up to the point where its retention does not interfere with the improvement of use of the artifact, but no further. In some cases, as with the pneumatic hammer, no aspect of the old form can be retained. In such cases, but in only such cases, should the form be determined solely on the basis of engineering efficiency.

In the cases we have been considering, the use to which the artifacts can be put are patent practical uses that can be understood intellectually and conceptually.

But apparently from the point of view we are expounding, there is more to the problem of form than its function to make observers unequivocally aware of such practical use.

Consider the case of a church. It is apparent that its general form should not be such that it looks like a factory. But more and beyond this, its form, especially its interior form, should make the beholder consciously aware of all the multiple potential purposes and urges that he can be cognizant of only intuitively, in the nature of value-qualities that have in his prior experiences been related to his satisfying use of places of worship. As I understand it, such forms are usually called "pure form" and the value-qualities related to them are called "beauty" (esthetic experience).

It would seem apparent that this so-called pure form is not an absolute characteristic, but is determined by the prior conditioning of the beholder. A Quaker is disturbed by the interior of a cathedral and a Catholic or Episcopalian is left cold by a Quaker meeting house.*

It would also seem apparent that "pure form" must be related to the purposes that are intellectually and logically understood by the beholder. Still further, it would seem apparent that if the value-qualities suggested by "pure form" were incongruous with the intellectual purposes that it would be worse than if no value-quality were suggested at all. That is, it would be easier for both Quaker and Catholic to worship in the woods than in the other's church.

What has been said above applies to what might be called public artifacts. That is, the "form" of tools and buildings used in common by the public should be such as to arouse visual awareness of potential purposes and value satisfactions common to the whole group, as in churches and meeting houses.

But when we consider form in its connection with artifacts for individual use, although the same basic principles apply, their application requires that the form must be varied to fit the unique purposes and value satisfactions of the particular individual. The "form" of a private house should be such as to arouse visual awareness in the owner

* At this point, since both Walker and Ames use the Quaker meeting house and the Roman Catholic church as examples, it is interesting to examine their different approaches to the value of architecture. Walker says (p. 76), " (man) molds . . . space to meet his immediate needs." Ames believes his experiments indicate that "man's highest artifact," by its form, can be a frustrating influence, or can help man "more successfully carry out his purposes in the direction of their evolutionary emergence."—Ed.

of his particular unique purposes and value satisfactions. For only insofar as man can experience emergence through the carrying out of his own purposes and the fulfilling of his own value satisfactions can he truly exist.

All of the foregoing leads us to a final and most important point that should be considered in regard to the responsibility of architects in planning man's physical environment. Our modern civilization is characterized by the rapidity with which new purposes and value-qualities both group and individual are emerging.

It would seem to follow that it is the responsibility of architects to be aware of the nature of these emergences and continually to provide new artifacts which will enable both groups and individuals to carry out their continually emerging purposes and create new emergent value-quality.

THE IMPORTANCE OF ORDER IN VISION

BY GYORGY KEPES

Designer, critic and educator, Mr. Kepes has had a strong influence on the understanding of form and the part that vision plays not only in esthetics but in the whole pattern of man's activities. His book, *The Language of Vision*, is referred to several times in this symposium, and is included in Walter Gropius' bibliography on page 173. Kepes is now teaching at the School of Architecture and Planning of the Massachusetts Institute of Technology.

THE dynamic basis of human beings is to form whatever situation they face into an integrated whole. Without ordering his reactions man cannot proceed to a new situation. Without ordering his physical environment he cannot survive. His creative capacity to construct his environment in terms of his needs, that is, to work out a relative equilibrium, is the very foundation of his existence.

Vision is a key example of this creative act of integration.

The eye faces a turmoil of light stimulations; light rays impinging on the retina have no intrinsic order as such; it is the dynamic need and tendency of the mind to find an order which transforms the sensuous basis into meaningful unities.

Vision, the orderer, receives its scope and scale from that which it orders. Visual experience is made up from the elements of the visible world around us. The strength, richness, and order of our visual forms depend on the nature of our visual surroundings.

If man sees a world around him in which the organic rhythm of nature's growth is revealed where colors, forms, and movements are expressions of organic events, then his vision becomes a true vision of reality based on a healthy foundation which Walt Whitman called the "primal sanities of nature." If the primal sanities of nature manifested by the variety of natural forms and events are absorbed through his vision, he is led to see, to look for, and demand them in the reshaping of his own man-made world.

Today we have lost this natural guidance, because we are embedded in a "second nature," in a man-shaped environment which could not grow naturally because it was intercepted and twisted by one-sided economic considerations. The appearance of things no longer reveals their nature—images take forms—forms cheat functions—functions are robbed of their natural sources—human needs. Urban landscapes, buildings with counterfeit insides and fake outsides, offices and factories, objects for use, the packaging of goods, the posters, the advertising in our newspapers, our clothes, our gestures, our physiognomy are without visual integrity. The world man has constructed is without sincerity, without scale, without cleanliness—twisted in space, without light and cowardly in color. It combines a mechanically precise pattern of the details within a formless whole. It is oppressive in its fake monumentality, it is degrading in its petty fawning manner of decorative face-lifting. Man, living in this false environment and injured emotionally and intellectually by the terrific odds of a chaotic society, cannot avoid having his sensibilities, the foundation of his creative faculty, impaired.

A man whose faculties are impaired narrows his world. He achieves a relative equilibrium in his environment only by artificially shrinking it in proportion to his difficulties. This impaired capacity is further characterized by lack of ability to make experience coherent. Today because this failing expresses itself as an inability to bring sensuous, emotional, and intellectual levels of experience to a single focus, a diffused image without cohesion prevents man's movements from one situation to another.

To bring direction and order to this formlessness we need to regain the health of our creative faculties, and not the least, of our visual sensibilities. As the nourishment of our vision is adulterated its only chance to regain health is to fast until the poison is digested, and until it restores its integrity. This was exactly what twentieth century visual art aimed at and partially achieved. Losing confidence in the adulterated visual surroundings, artists restrained themselves from using the visible world as their material. They returned to the only genuine visual source, which still kept the sanities of nature, to the creative tendency of the eye to see visual "wholes." Painters and sculptors, because of their distrust of their familiar surroundings, cleaned their respective media of everything which in the least resembled these surroundings. In their consistent search they reached a truth which they called the "plastic truth," an integrated vision, realized in terms of the material in which they worked. This vision, becoming nature again because of its organic quality, must now re-enter our physical environment. Order, structural unity, must guide the shaping of our surroundings and thus restore them to true nature again—a higher nature because they are impregnated with human understanding. A visual control of the environment guided by healthy vision would give man not only a sounder physical setting but also, what is as important, it would reinstate his creative continuity and thus increase his stature. Instead of giving a sheer palpability of usefulness through its genuine visual forms, this new environment could generate a new imagery, a new symbolic form of basic human values.

ESTHETICS AS HARMONIOUS FULFILLMENT

BY ARTHUR C. HOLDEN

Two brief statements are inserted in the discussion at this point to indicate several of the points of discussion which are bound to arise when translation of the theories of form development into actual design becomes necessary. Arthur Holden, architect, worries lest we think in two-dimensional terms only, and points out again that esthetics cannot be applied. A. M. Friend, Jr., of Princeton's Department of Art and Archeology, fears that we will forget solid substances in our concern with space use.

IT IS pertinent to inquire why we admit, as readily as we do, that man is better off when he lives and works in an environment which has esthetic values. In the first place, where does this esthetic value come from? For myself, I do not believe that esthetic value can be created through conscious aim. Esthetic value is the evidence of an innate harmony that has been achieved through the arrangement of space in such a way that human needs and senses are satisfied.

Too frequently in judging esthetic values overemphasis is placed upon aspect. This gives rise to visual aberrations and exaggerations. Instead of achieving harmony in three dimensions, many designs are worked out in two dimensions only. Sometimes two-dimensional emphasis is given to a plan in a horizontal plane, sometimes two-dimensional emphasis is given to a composition in a vertical plane or elevation. The solids and the voids are the things that men feel, rather than the arrangement of lines.

Environment can be molded so that it creates or stimulates a mood. It may be formal or informal, intimate or austere; it may be romantic, or it may follow the modern tendency to be dramatic.

Through design natural environment is developed or changed to suit man's purposes. Again, I say that esthetic satisfactions are produced as a result of the harmonious coordination of the factors which make up the design. Good architecture is fundamentally related to its social purpose and the landscape. The experienced mind can recognize the harmonious fulfillment of a design which satisfies man's needs. Unfortunately, the inexperienced mind has not seen enough of good design to be sensitive to disharmony.

VOIDS AND SOLIDS

BY A. M. FRIEND, JR.

THE point has been made that the use of space gives value to the solids of architecture; this is a relatively modern remark. In earlier architecture the solids gave meaning to the voids. Actually, just as in the development of true landscape in painting, in architecture at relatively the same time—i.e., the Baroque period—space begins to rule the solid forms. Today the development of spacial elements and the relation of different kinds of space, static and in motion, has been wonderfully exploited, as in works by Frank Lloyd Wright and others. But the solids have been neglected until sometimes the only relationship between solid and void is an antithetic one which is violent and absolute. Thus the vocabulary of architecture, forms which relate solid and void, has been seriously reduced. No new system of forms has arisen to replace the columns, consoles, volutes, moldings of the old architecture thus to free the solids and allow modern architecture to resolve the dichotomy of sheer geometry versus natural space. It is by a "humanizing" of the solids that architecture will advance to a really expressive style.

JOSEPH HUDNUT

ARCHITECTURAL VALUES

BY JOSEPH HUDNUT

This and the next paper in this section deal with the philosophical aspects of form. Joseph Hudnut, who here speaks of the complex of values that must be considered in judging architecture, is Dean of the Graduate School of Design at Harvard University. Dean Hudnut has had an active life as educator, practitioner, and writer on architecture. Under his aegis the School at Harvard has become one of the most progressive in the country.

WHENEVER we judge architecture we are confronted by a confusing complexity of values: technological, esthetic, social, and philosophical. Like electrons in a molecule, these may assume an almost infinite range of structure, movement, and relationship.

In an era saturated with technological thought, buildings will be judged by technological standards. We will ask how buildings are put together, how they work, and in what way the energies of their materials react against each other. Buildings will be judged as chairs or clocks or airplanes are judged.

Just the same, we cannot—even if we wished to do so—exclude esthetic valuations. We are not satisfied without proportion, rhythmic relationship, harmonies in texture and color. Willy-nilly the bases of our judgments will shift from technologies to these, the more ancient criteria of architecture. We have not forgotten that the art of building is, like painting and music, a fine art.

The times, meanwhile, have made us social-minded. Beyond organism and appearances we look for those values which have their origins in the commerce of society. We judge buildings by that which they contribute to social health and the general good, by the way in which they sustain our cultural traditions and our forward march. We like schoolhouses better than country houses, cathedrals better than garages, planned cities better than slums.

All of these are valid judgments. The confusions they engender—and the conflicts—arise from changes in our intellectual preoccupations and in our ways of seeing, and these in turn are shaped for us by the currents of thought and the circumstances of our time.

Only one valuation remains constant. Architecture, whether considered as engineering, esthetic satisfaction, or social service, is always an art of expression. Nothing is built without philosophy; nor is there any building which can be judged apart from the man who created it, from his vision of the universe, and the ideals which he entertained. Our buildings tell us not only what we value in architecture but what we value in human life.

That is why I should have every architect a speculator in things of the spirit. The worth-whileness of man, the dignity of his institutions, and his destiny on this earth ought to be the persistent themes of our art, more closely pressed than any other against the heart of the world. It is important that these meanings should be made eloquent in the buildings which we build and the cities which we plan.

THE PHILOSOPHY OF FORM

BY THEODORE M. GREENE

One of the unusual aspects of this discussion is that it brings to the same forum architects, psychologists, educators, teachers of art, and philosophers. Professor Greene, of Yale University's Department of Philosophy, has given much thought to the philosophy of art creation and art criticism. He has taught at the University of Punjab, in India, and at Princeton. His books include *The Arts and the Art of Criticism* (1940) and *The Meaning of the Humanities* (1938).

His thesis that "architecture transcends mere engineering and the requirements of mere utility" leads him to somewhat the same conclusion that Ames has found: "It is (the architect's) responsibility to lead the way . . . toward the eradication of human frustration and the enrichment of human life. . . ."

I WILL not waste time telling you how much I don't know about architecture. That will become all too evident as I proceed. My job is to try to contribute something to your deliberations in my dual capacity, as a layman who is somewhat sensitive to his architectural environment, and as a philosopher who has given some attention to some of the central problems of architecture. Let me try to summarize in the ten minutes at my disposal my conception of these basic problems. I shall not try to be original; I shall try, rather, to formulate the larger issues as I see them in such a way as to lay a foundation and erect a framework for your subsequent discussion.

What is architecture? It is both a many-sided and an organically unified phenomenon. Buildings are, first of all, physical structures erected on physical sites to satisfy various physical human needs. It is axiomatic that this physical dimension is basic to architecture and must never be neglected or minimized. On the contrary, architecture at its best has always gloried in these physical factors and exploited them to the full, openly and joyously.

This physical side of architecture and of man is, of course, the special province of engineering, on the one hand, the social studies, on the other. To proclaim the importance of these physical factors is therefore to recognize the continual relevance of engineering, in all its ramifications, and of economics and politics, finance and medicine, to the overall problem of architecture. All the corporate activities of human beings—familial and industrial, academic, civic, and religious—which architecture must attempt to house have their inescapable physical aspects, and it is these which constitute such basic necessities as heat and light, circulation and storage, space for larger and smaller groups, and for solitary work and leisure. How to satisfy these needs as ingeniously and economically as possible is an ever-present challenge to the architect in his role as engineer.

If this were the whole story, however, architecture would not be one of the major arts; it would be identical with utilitarian engineering. Even as an art, architecture must do the fullest justice to these engineering and utilitarian factors; it must develop out of them and exploit them to the full; but it must also transcend them through its own distinctive genius. This new factor, which distinguishes architecture from mere engineering, brings us to the heart of our problem.

Architecture *must* transcend engineering because the human activities which it houses are not merely physical and utilitarian in the narrower sense, but also, and significantly, cultural and spiritual. Family life, the processes of government, education and research, religious worship, and even business and industry as responsible and dignified human activities, all involve human relationships, human values and evaluations, cultural traditions and standards, spiritual aspirations. To ignore these is to reduce man to his merely physical components and acts; to recognize and promote them is the distinctive task of architecture as an art.

Architecture *can* recognize and promote man's cultural and spiritual welfare because a building can achieve, in its visible texture and structure, its control of solids and spaces, a visible form which is not only intrinsically satisfying but which, in addition, is expressive of the emotions, feelings, and moods characteristic of the human activities which the building houses. This has been so universally acknowledged that it hardly needs to be further demonstrated, but two illustrations may clarify what I mean.

A few years ago I defended the thesis, before a group of theologians, that the arts, in conjunction, constitute the languages of public religious worship. This thesis was challenged by the late Professor Rufus Jones, the distinguished Quaker, on the ground that a Quaker meeting has no need for any of the arts. "But would you," I said to Mr. Jones, "just as willingly worship God in the manner of the Friends in an ugly barn as in a fine old Quaker Meeting House whose architecture so eloquently expresses the austerity and sincerity of a Friends' meeting?" Whereupon he ad-

mitted that such a building would make a valuable contribution to their religious worship. My other illustration is
as direct and self-explanatory as a good caricature. What
sort of private dwelling would seem to you to be appropriate to Wallace Beery, of Hollywood fame? Not, I venture to believe, the elegant eighteenth-century French villa,
complete with formal garden and fountain, which was
pointed out to me in 1940 as his current domicile!

In short, architecture transcends mere engineering and
the requirements of mere utility in proportion as its visible surface, interior and exterior, and the controlled space,
express, in the language of an appropriate style, what I
venture to call the cultural and spiritual, in distinction
from the merely physical, aspects of the human activities
which the building houses.

If this analysis is correct, the architect has today, as always, the two complementary problems of "program" and
"plan"—the problem of how to diagnose man's needs, and
the problem of how to offer his distinctive architectural
contribution to the satisfaction of these needs through expressive architectural form.

To satisfy the ideal requirements of his profession he
must, on the one hand, be a profound student of human
nature, mindful of enduring human traits, but equally
mindful of the ever-changing course of human history. He
must be sensitive to present-day necessities and aspirations,
but he must understand these in the perspective of the past.
To know only the present is to be merely contemporary;
to be truly modern is to see the present and to plan for the
future in the context of past failures and achievements. He
must also be aware of the generic character of human activities and institutions, secular and religious; yet he must be
no less aware of the unique requirements of his particular
client or clients. He must be partly guided by their demands; yet he must also try to understand them better than
they understand themselves and to build for them with an
eye to their potential future development and to their
later needs of which they may themselves still be unaware.

His "plan," in turn, must develop *pari passu* with his diagnosis of his "program." Here his problem is essentially the problem of style. How can he, in terms of his own artistic individuality and of the times in which he is living, make the fullest use of available building materials and modern engineering principles and create a language of architectural forms which will express the spirit and temper of man's perennial yet ever-changing corporate activities? He can count, I believe, on the gradual awakening of the public to the expressive power of the new forms which he creates. As Mr. Ames has demonstrated in his work in Dartmouth, what we actually "see" in ordinary perception is only partly dictated by immediate sensation; we perceive what we have learned to perceive in the manner in which we have unconsciously learned to perceive it, and for the satisfaction of our needs and purposes. This means that we are all susceptible to education, including esthetic education in the evolving expressive languages of the arts. The architect's task, then, is not merely to use to the full whatever architectural languages are available to him from older generations, but, in addition, to modify or even revolutionize these languages insofar as the modern temper requires it and insofar as his inventiveness can create the required new architectural forms.

It is on this theme that Mr. Giedion's historical studies are so significant, for he is concerned with architecture as a living and evolving art, forever rooted in engineering, yet forever transcending mere engineering in its concern for form which at once expresses and evokes human feeling. And it is in this context that such problems as the nature of scale become acute—scale as a purely physical, quantitative phenomenon, measurable in feet and inches; scale as an esthetic fact, of balance and proportion, as, for example, in the Greek Orders; and, finally, scale as an architectural expression of the human spirit, of triviality or dignity, of secular or religious aspiration in this or that culture. I hope you will discuss precisely how these aspects of scale are related to each other. How can the esthetic evolve out of the quantitative, and the expressive out of the esthetic? This, I submit, is typical of the strictly architectural problems which transcend mere engineering, dependent though their solution is on engineering principles.

I will conclude with a word of exhortation and a word of caution. Both as a layman and as a philosopher I would exhort you not to underrate your prophetic function. It is indeed your responsibility to lead the way, in city planning, in domestic architecture, in industrial construction and design, towards the eradication of human frustration and the enrichment of human life in all its housed activities. But—and this is my word of caution—you cannot accomplish this singlehanded. Only in close cooperation with the wisest and most forward-looking artists and scientists, political, social, and religious leaders, industrialists and businessmen and scholars in our society, can architecture hope really to satisfy man's needs, physical and spiritual, individual and collective, contemporary and enduring. Leaders in other fields will always need your help as imaginative and socially sensitive architects. You will always need their help both for a fuller understanding of man and society, and for the difficult task of guiding a lethargic society into better ways of human living.

ESTHETIC VALUES

BY SIGFRIED GIEDION

Dr. Giedion, author of the well-known and influential *Space, Time and Architecture*, as well as many other works (his *Mechanization Takes Command*, several chapters from which have been printed in magazines here and abroad, was issued in 1948 by the Oxford University Press) is an internationally known architectural historian and critic. As an active member of CIAM he has been in the forefront of the modern movement, a protagonist of full utilization of the possibilities of the machine age and also, as this paper indicates, much concerned with the emotional and esthetic implications of architecture and planning.

Giedion's paper is saved for the last in this section, because it leads naturally into the discussion of education which follows. He sums up very nearly all that has been said before: Esthetic values cannot be arbitrarily applied; esthetic sensations have an impact on man's decisions; human needs dominate. But, he says, "We have to prepare the next generation." Education—education of society to the possibilities open, and education of the architect to "realize the social, moral, and emotional demands" of the work ahead of him—that, to Dr. Giedion, is now the all-important thing.

THERE can be no doubt that the purpose of this session is to look beyond the utilitarian and functional values of the human environment and to assume the existence of esthetic and spiritual values.

To begin with, we don't believe that esthetic values can be arbitrarily added to or subtracted from an object. Esthetic values are inherent in things.* They emanate from them, just as odors do from food or from flowers. And like these intangible perfumes they determine our sensitive or emotional reaction.

Esthetic impacts influence us at all moments. Consciously, or in most cases subconsciously, they provoke friendly or hostile reactions. They escape from our rationalistic strongholds, directly back to our emotions and therefore out of our control.

This means esthetic values are no simple trimmings but indeed have their roots in the depth of the soul. Their impact on man's decisions reaches even into the most practical problems, into the shaping of things of daily use—cars, bridges, and above all, our human environment.

* Nothing indicates more clearly than this recurring statement the contribution to esthetics that the Ames studies may in time make. When Dr. Giedion makes the statement, which is a modern one, that esthetic values are "inherent in things," he is not in purposeful conflict with Ames's conclusion that visual sensations "are not inherent in the so-called external 'things' at which we are looking." It simply indicates that there is the possibility of a readjustment (with huge implications) of our understanding of what, in things and in man, really produces the esthetic experience. The broader realization that it is a combination of background and personal history that causes things to look as they do to the people who see them merely implements Dr. Giedion's argument as he develops it.—Ed.

If man's esthetic or, as we would prefer to express it, if man's emotional needs are not satisfied, he will react immediately. He will reject most violently the slightest deviation from his esthetic standards. He will do everything in his power to shape things according to his emotional convictions.

Here is an example: We have in Switzerland the case of Robert Maillart, the bridgebuilder who died without the opportunity to erect in any of our cities an arch in the pure forms which he mastered like no one else. His bridges were permitted only in remote mountain valleys, because they were cheap and, above all, because nobody was supposed to see them. Why? Their extreme lightness and elegance offended the taste of the laymen and the specialists, who hated their soaring strength. We have had enough of these puff-pastry bridges, said one of them.

In Berne, where Maillart's bridges had to span the river Aare, he was forced to disguise them completely with heavy granite stonework, thus annihilating his own elegance. Because of their emotional training, the officials preferred massive bridges. It made no difference whatsoever that this massiveness was very costly, because their emotional needs were satisfied.

Today we can observe this astonishing dictatorship of esthetic values or emotional needs in every country. One can admire the officials concerned with building parks and highway systems for the keenness of their conceptions, but the moment they have to do with architecture their keenness vanishes. We then see them clinging anxiously to nineteenth-century habits. This is a world-wide official disease.

The emotional training of the average man lags far behind the advanced nature of his thinking. The whole disaster of nineteenth-century architecture is based in a large degree on this divergence. And, as T. S. Eliot says, "The nineteenth century still lingers on into the twentieth."

In our period, feeling seems to be much more difficult than thinking. Mankind is able today to invent nearly everything it wants in science, and make all kinds of gadgets. But, as soon as you approach the emotional, or if you prefer, the esthetic sphere, you will immediately meet the strongest resistance.

This was not always so. It was often the reverse. Artists like Michelangelo, in spite of their keen and revolutionary inventions, were conscripted by the Pope, like present-day atom physicists by the Government. But scientific thinkers like Galileo were condemned and outlawed for their discoveries, just as today we exclude the inventors in the emotional field, called creative artists, from public activity. The result is that the esthetic values born out of the spirit of our period are ignored.

Today the immediate impact of the esthetical or emotional values has grown to the utmost importance. Why? Suddenly we have become aware of our predicament. Suddenly and unavoidably, human needs have to dominate the problems of production.

The task ahead of us seems nearly impossible and yet we must accomplish it. We must simultaneously shape elements and synthesis. Town planning, the highest expression of architectural synthesis, is normally mastered at the peak, or even at the end, of an era. So it was in Greece. So it was in the thirteenth century with its frantic founding of cities. And so it was in the late eighteenth century when urbanism of the highest spatial order was within the reach of every speculator.

But what happens today? Building techniques, as compared with other techniques, are lagging behind. How should people be housed? Flats, single houses? The very existence of the city itself is questioned. Look at the esthetic uncertainty on the drawing boards the moment a larger synthesis is required, as in civic centers. And yet we have to work simultaneously at the beginning and at the end. For there is a revolt in the making, a revolt which can no longer be suppressed. This is the revolt of the humiliated human instincts.

May I draw a pertinent conclusion? We have to prepare the next generation for these enormous tasks lying ahead.

The present curricula are insufficiently adjusted to the necessities of this period. The students feel it strongly, sometimes more strongly than their professors. In every country the same question pops up. "How should our training be organized so that we may realize the social, moral, and emotional demands of our work?"

I will illustrate from my own field. History is often forced on students as if nothing had happened in architecture for the last hundred years. History is taught as if it were static, not dynamic. But history is dynamic. The past lives in us and acts in us. As Henri Bergson, the French philosopher whose shadow looms larger with the years, puts it, "The past gnaws relentlessly into the future." We must forge history into a weapon which will enable the coming generation to measure where they stand, to judge their strength and their weaknesses.

SECTION IV

EDUCATION

INTRODUCTION

BY THOMAS H. CREIGHTON

T HE fourth session at the Princeton Conference was reserved for a review and additional discussion of the topics covered in the first three: the social, physical, and intellectual attributes of design. A number of the comments, though interesting or amusing, were scarcely worth preserving; the American Institute of Architects was defended against a charge that had been made, accusing it of not dealing firmly with the social and political aspects of housing and planning. Frank Lloyd Wright attended this gathering (the only one at which he was present, except for the final dinner where he spoke) and provided a diversion by explaining, gratuitously, the difference between the Oriental and the Occidental mind. The Western intellectual approach is one of directness, he said (using a blackboard at the front of the room and drawing a straight line between two points). The Eastern approach is a circuitous one, he explained (drawing a curve beginning at the first point, surrounding but impinging on the far point), which reaches its object more slowly, but in a manner which gives it more experience and a broader vision. Then before he sat down he asked irrelevantly, "What is this AIA you have been talking about—this *union?*"

Wright drew two responses. Roland Wank asked whether the attack on Pearl Harbor had been an example of the roundabout or the direct approach to an end. And George Howe explained the AIA. It believes in a code of professional ethics, he said, which goes like this—and he traced Wright's circular Oriental line. But, he said, it also recognizes the principle of self-protection, and that goes like this —drawing over the straight line of Occidental directness.

Aside from these relaxations, however, most of the discussion that evening had to do with architectural education. Although no session of the Conference had been assigned specifically to this subject, the original Bicentennial

Announcement, calling the series of conferences of which this was one, had said, "Princeton . . . proposes to direct its Bicentennial Celebration to the end of applying, in consultation with scholars throughout the world, our common skills, knowledge, and wisdom to the fundamental obligations of higher learning to human society. . . ." With a large number of educators present, it was inevitable that this matter should have come to the fore. The various statements concerned with education have, therefore, been gathered together in this part of the book, and other things that may have been said on that evening have either been omitted or placed elsewhere, where they seemed more appropriate.

The papers in this section recognize the fact that remarkable changes and improvements in architectural education have been made in recent years, but they also call attention to the inconsistency and lack of direction in this advance. The most obvious complaint—that mere elimination of the training which was based on copying "styles" is not enough, unless it is replaced by something more vital—is the premise from which all the discussion springs. As Dr. Giedion says, "In the nineteenth century . . . students were trained to regard the past as a warehouse of forms, where one could borrow or pilfer *ad libitum*." But, pointed out Richard Bennett before the meeting:

I am eager to see steps taken which will . . . above all make it clear that students *following* a modern "style" are not necessarily superior to students *following* any other style. The employment of fashionable form in the contemporary esthetic manner does not automatically prove the possession of, nor is it anywhere nearly so important as, an understanding of the *broad* problem of architecture.

Henry Kamphoefner agreed, and added:

If we try to develop students with strong intellectual capacities, giving them sound historical and philosophical understanding of architecture, will we not come out with young students who will work for an indigenous and *organic* architecture? Style will then be integral. That kind of student, I believe, will have too much integrity to be an eclectic and work in "any other style." At the same time such a student, as a true scholar of architecture searching for the truth in his work, would be too humble to consider himself "superior" to the eclectic who works in "any other style."

None of the critics or historians who have insisted on the appropriateness of the appellation, "International Style," or who have more recently invented the terms, "International Cottage Style" and "The New Empiricism," were present at the Conference. Hence there was no further worrying of this point, but rather an acceptance of the fact that educational as well as design criteria should be based on history, social understanding, technical knowledge, and esthetic principles rather than a self-conscious concern with either old or new "styles."

The questions remained, however, just how that "sound historical and philosophical understanding of architecture" which Bennett spoke of should be inculcated. There is the matter of teaching space-use, there is the matter of teaching structures, there is the need for the various subdivisions of the design professions to understand something of one another's problems, there is the teaching of planning and the teaching of the psychology of vision—above all, there is the controlling problem which Dr. Giedion points to, of teaching to the architectural student "his future role of a *coordinator*, so that he may be enabled to integrate the elements supplied by specialized knowledge into a *work of art*."

The discussion at the end of this section, supplied by Dr. Giedion, is actually a postscript to the Princeton Conference. As he explains, a resolution on education was proposed in all good faith, but was ruled out of order—not because the chairman disagreed with what it said, but because it seemed inconsistent with the academic nature of the meeting. Hence it was signed by many of the participants and forwarded to UNESCO as an independent expression, in the hope that some concrete results might come of the gathering together of so many people concerned with architectural education. It resulted eventually in the concluding paper in this section, a memorandum of Dr. Giedion's to UNESCO, which has not otherwise appeared in print.

The sequence of the discussion is simple. First Kenneth Kassler, who was chairman of Session IV, reviews the three preceding sessions and translates the conclusions that have been drawn into educational terms. Then follow several papers discussing various individual apects of the problem of teaching architecture. Then finally comes the resolution and its result, as at least a start toward some international action on proper curricula.

THE NEED FOR EXPLAINING
OUR AIMS

BY KENNETH KASSLER

Architect and sometime instructor in architecture, Kenneth Kassler believes that the training of architects is as important as the accomplishment of successful work, of which he has done his share. It was his job at the Conference to act as discussion leader of the session which summed up the first three. His remarks in introducing the discussion act as an excellent introduction also to this section of the book.

IN SUMMARY of the papers up to this point, certain thoughts appear to be generally common to the statements and ensuing discussions. Of these, perhaps the most dominant is the idea that "man" is the unit of measure around which architecture should be imagined and conceived. This might sound commonplace and trite since man remains always at the focal point of our activities. What is meant, however, is a revitalization, or perhaps more exactly, a reorientation toward what we mean when we speak of "man" or "mankind." If I interpreted Dr. Morgan's re-

KENNETH KASSLER

marks correctly, this significant attitude can be inferred from his statement of the benefits which would result from a *full* acceptance of the democratic spirit in architecture. Andre Malraux, the French writer, sums it up succinctly when he says: "The essential task of our time is to establish our idea of man. This may seem nothing. Yet it is undoubtedly the most important problem for contemporary thought." Thus it would appear from the discussions that the recent emphasis on technological advances in architectural fields has been replaced somewhat by the importance newly assigned to the social, visual, and spiritual needs of mankind.

I should like to quote from Elton Mayo's book, *The Social Problems of an Industrial Civilization*. Professor Mayo is a member of the Department of Industrial Research of the Graduate School of Business Administration of Harvard University. His studies, seemingly far removed from architecture, do impinge upon the same problems confronting architects and planners.

"These studies (referring to industrial surveys made by Mayo) showed that the human desire for cooperative activity still persists in the ordinary person, even in communities of social chaos, and can be utilized by intelligent and skilled management. The administrator who achieves collaboration is one who recognizes the true source and nature of 'authority' and who looks upon his function as essentially one of receiving and understanding communications from others and acting in terms of social realities."

Since collaboration is an essential element in planning and architecting today, and since collaboration must be based on communication and understanding, we might well ponder Mr. Mayo's remarks in relation to architectural education.

Louis Justement, in a conversation after Session III, emphasized the necessity of being able to impart our professional information to those not equally well versed in our own terminology. We must make ourselves clear to those for whom we wish to plan, as well as to those men and

· 111 ·

women who are now students but later will be architects and planners. One of the main tasks which architects and planners living in this age must acknowledge is that of understanding its needs, and more importantly, of making their efforts and aims understood by the laymen. Both of these problems should be constant focal points of attention and study in our architectural education.

THE NEED FOR A
STRUCTURAL VOCABULARY

BY HENRY KAMPHOEFNER

At the time of the Conference, Kamphoefner was a professor in the School of Architecture of the University of Oklahoma. Since then he has taken up new duties as Dean of the newly constituted School of Architecture and Landscape Design at North Carolina State College. Like Kassler, he has been interested both in the practice and the teaching of integrated design, but his time has been spent almost exclusively, in recent years, as an educator. While at Oklahoma, he and the staff which worked with him spent much thought and effort on the integral teaching of structure to the beginning student, with remarkable success. His interest in this paper is toward a wider concern with this aspect of training in the schools.

THE development of architectural education during the last two decades is related to many changes in the understanding of significant form. There have been advances in the study and the discipline of the functions of our buildings and in the matter of good proportions, or the esthetics of a building. However, the achievement of original and imaginative form through a full knowledge and understanding of basic structure has been neglected in the teaching of most of the schools.

All progressive schools now know that the student must learn proportion more freely than the hackneyed "rendering of the orders" permitted. A feeling for good proportion, we find, can be taught best by work in basic design studies; a book such as *The Language of Vision*, by Gyorgy Kepes, has been of value as a primer in showing the young student methods for creating good design, well proportioned. Three dimensional studies have also been added to replace the old work in descriptive geometry. The fact remains that most of our schools have not found a way to give the young student a fundamental structural vocabulary during his very earliest work.

It is true that we are coordinating our work in design with construction much better than ever before, but our schools must learn to familiarize the beginning student at the earliest possible stage of his development with that basic structural vocabulary. By the time the advanced work in structural analysis is understood by the student, his creative habits have been partially crystallized and he tends to let the handbook limit him. If he acquires a structural vocabulary at an early age, even though it is implemented by nothing but simple rule-of-thumb procedures or a survey of the possibilities and limitations of the basic systems of structure, then structural form plays an integral role in his entire architectural development and growth.

In our historical studies we have learned what the negation of structure did to the architecture of the Renaissance. On the other hand, we have examples in past periods, such as the Gothic, of an understanding and use of structural form, and in our own day Frank Lloyd Wright's greatest work, based on unique intuitive structural ideas, shows us to what heights architecture can go when structural understanding is integral with all phases of the creative process.

THE VALUES OF VISUAL EDUCATION

BY FRED N. SEVERUD

A consulting engineer with a rare understanding of the entire design process, Fred Severud was born in Norway, earned his degree at the National Institute of Technology in Trondheim, and came to the United States in 1923. In his practice he has developed several important construction methods, and in his published papers he has done much for the coordination of "engineering" and "architecture." He has served as consultant to the Government of Puerto Rico and technical adviser to the Norwegian Government.

In this paper Severud argues the value of visual aids—particularly movie "shorts" as a means for teaching each branch of the designing professions sufficient of the technical bases of the others so that full coordination can result.

I BELIEVE most of us will agree that there is an ever-widening gap between the onrush of knowledge in architectural and technical fields and the assimilation of knowledge through education. The result has been that the knowledge is cut up into small enough pieces for specialized professions to absorb. That this trend can be stopped or reversed is questionable, but I feel very strongly that an overall understanding can be achieved and that the work of the specialists can become more coordinated than at present.

Certain basic principles occur and re-occur throughout all aspects of the provision of the proper physical environment for man. If those fundamental principles could be mastered by all the designing professions alike, they would serve to link them together in a mutual understanding of the purposes and problems that each is striving for or is confronted with.

I believe it is well recognized that it would be desirable for the architect, as coordinator, to master all these basic fundamentals. It is not so well recognized, however, that his consultants should also have a basic knowledge of all phases of the construction field. Planning man's physical environment should be a common venture. It should be quite obvious then that if it were possible for all who are engaged in this venture to agree on a common denominator of basic principles, better coordination throughout would result. It is also evident, I think, that on the basis of an understanding of fundamentals in the entire field, each one of the specialists could contribute valuable thoughts even in the fields other than his own, due to looking at the problem from various angles.

But how can specialists so desperately intent on absorbing the knowledge within their own fields be expected to spend much time and effort in reviewing others? It is obvious that since our days and weeks cannot be stretched, we must look for more efficient means of imparting knowledge.

It would be very unreasonable indeed if the tremendous efforts made in winning the war, by the United States in particular, did not leave in their wake some valuable pointers. Time was of the essence. Soldiers had to learn, and learn fast. The best brains of the country were put to work to cut through the old educational methods and devise others that would bring results more quickly. Methods of using film and sound proved to be marvelously effective. By these means the soldiers were equipped to meet the exigencies of the battlefield in record time.

Many recognize that similar methods can be used by our schools in peace time. However, I do not think it is fully realized that by dramatizing the very essence of a structure, a much more live and accurate conception could be obtained of the tools that we are working with. Let me take an example from my own field, where we are concerned with moments, shears, reinforcement, stirrups, tension, compression. Mastery of words and definitions often makes a student believe that he knows the basic principles. Then if he learns formulae by heart and is able to solve some problems mathematically, he may feel that he has acquired worth-while knowledge. If, however, this knowledge is superficial, it is of small value indeed.

Let us suppose that a movie were made showing a reinforced concrete beam that had collapsed. The main piece would be lying on the floor, and jagged parts would still be stuck to the columns. By portraying the hoisting back again of the broken piece, sewing it up with stirrups, putting in the proper elements to prevent it from pulling away again at the top of the break and from being crushed at the bottom of the break, the basic principles of a beam could be portrayed so dramatically that they would never be forgotten. An intelligent commentator and a clever cartoonist could portray the efforts and struggles of little imps doing the work, and an interesting ten minutes spent watching the picture would leave a lasting impression. Another movie "short" that could be made would demonstrate various structural forms in nature. Structure could be dramatized by the breaking of a blade of grass or the branch of a tree.

Visual education would be very useful also in highlighting certain important types of construction. Construction methods as well as structural systems could be indelibly impressed upon eye and ear by intelligent selection and dramatic presentation of the material used. If, in short, an effort would be made to free the students from the straitjacket of terms and definitions and words, and give them a basic new feeling of the fascinating interplay of gravitational and physical forces, they would maintain a solid platform from which to view the specialized fields long after they had forgotten all of the formulae.

I am well enough aware of the difficulties in instituting a program of this kind, but I feel convinced that if an intelligent start is made, it will not be very long until educational methods are driven in this direction by their own inertia. My experience in lecturing has convinced me that the greatest interest is aroused when an effort is made to introduce the audience visually to basic fundamentals.

THE COST OF VISUAL AIDS

BY LEOPOLD ARNAUD

Dean of the School of Architecture at Columbia University, Leopold Arnaud engaged in the practice of architecture between the time that he graduated from the École des Beaux Arts and entered the profession of teaching. He is a member of the AIA as well as the Société des Architectes Diplomés par le Gouvernement Francaise. He looks with a practical eye at the advantages—and costs—of visual aids in the teaching of architecture.

IT IS evident that a greater use of visual aids would improve the teaching of architecture in many ways. We already have the technical skill to help us and I might say that we also have the imagination; what is lacking is the financial help.

Not so very many years ago when lantern slides became available, the budget outlay necessary to purchase slides and lanterns was not excessive. Most schools now have adequate collections of black and white slides, used mostly in connection with the teaching of architectural history, and a modest budget for upkeep and improvement is usually obtainable.

But recent improvements in visual material have shown us the great advantages which can be derived from their use: color, always important to the architect, but especially so to the contemporary designer, can now be shown; three-dimensional representations can clarify the teaching of descriptive geometry, construction, and drawing; moving pictures can contribute greatly to visualization, and can demonstrate, in a clearer way than ever before, the assembly of parts and the sequences of manufacture. Furthermore, diagrammatic movies can illustrate many things which even the best teachers cannot explain on the blackboard.

These advantages are known to us all, but the great stumbling block at present is the expense, especially the expense of making the material—movies, colored slides, or assemblages. The schools have given this matter much thought, but so far they have not been able to solve the problem of cost.

During the war the Government could spend large sums for the development of short movies for the instruction of the troops; much was learned about the advantages and disadvantages of this type of training. But schools for pro-

fessionals do not have the same needs as the Government
in time of war, nor do they have the same sums available.

The development of these visual aids could, to some
extent, be a joint problem for all of the schools, perhaps
through the Association of Collegiate Schools of Architecture which has already done some study along these lines.*
But each school would also have its own specific requirements which could not be covered by group service.

Much could be done, much should be done. The question is: Where is the money coming from?

THE NEED FOR A BASIC REFORM
IN ARCHITECTURAL EDUCATION

BY SIGFRIED GIEDION

Dr. Giedion, who was introduced in this book by his paper on
esthetic values on page 99, has always been concerned with the
methods, as well as the results, of architectural education. As
a historian and teacher of architectural history, he has no use
for the teaching of history by "elaborating a false continuity
from the Stone Age to the twentieth century." He feels sure
that "we want to know, in the manner of biologists, how the
life of a culture took place."

Dr. Giedion, along with others at the Conference, felt that
a complete restudy of the basis of architectural education and
the necessary curricula was indicated by the discussion. Since
the UNESCO, established for the purpose of exploring such matters on a world-wide scale, was soon to hold an important meeting in Mexico, these participants felt it to be appropriate for
a memorandum to issue from the Conference urging that body,
under Dr. Julian Huxley, to concern itself with education in
architecture and planning. Passage of a "resolution" was ruled
out of order, but the suggestion did have further results, as Dr.
Giedion describes below.

* Wayne University has announced recently an Audio-visual Materials
Consultation Bureau, under the direction of Dr. Arthur Stenius, to give
advice by such means as "surveys showing school needs, critical analysis
of scripts and copy, and actual classroom tryout of material in 'rough' or
finished form."—Ed.

AFTER I had made my last point in the prepared paper on Esthetic Values at the Princeton Conference (page 99) I still had two minutes of my time left. Since I had arrived at a mention of architectural education, I went on, saying that, if we do not agree with the point of view that all teaching of architecture is to be rejected, then the spirit and the methods of this training remain of fundamental importance for the development of architecture. Although it must be admitted that the training has improved in many schools since the nineteenth century, when all vision was destroyed at its very roots, we are still meticulously teaching a considerable number of insufficiently integrated auxiliary sciences; we are still too close, I am afraid, to drawing-board architecture; we still fail to preserve and foster the original creative gifts of the student, and to bring him in close contact with the emotional currents which created a new art in our century. Therefore, I proposed the assembly to draw up a letter to Dr. Julian Huxley, Director General of the UNESCO, Paris, asking him to appoint a committee of professionals which should draft a plan for a basic reform of architectural education.

I was not at all aware at the moment that, by proposing this, I was infringing the rules, the purpose of the Princeton Conferences being limited to general orientation and exchange of ideas, without the intention to come to conclusions or to resolutions. The following letter was therefore written and signed outside the assembly hall. But, as it had some positive consequences, it may be regarded nevertheless as one of the fruitful outcomes of the Princeton Conference. The letter reads as follows:

The undersigned, met together at the Conference on "Planning Man's Physical Environment" on the occasion of the Bicentennial Celebration at Princeton University, urge that you set up immediately a committee of professionals and educators in the field of Planning and Architecture, to draw up a plan for a fundamental reform of training for Architects and Planners in all countries, and to draft as part of such a plan basic curricular standards for all countries.

This request is based on our conviction that existing curricula, with few exceptions, are not adjusted to the needs of the immense task of replanning and reconstruction which lies ahead of us everywhere.

We desire to state in particular that any new program must include development of knowledge of social, economic, and emotional factors involved as well as technical competence—for it is through the understanding of the interrelation of these that the Architect and Planner of our time may be properly equipped not only to make his special contribution more significant but further to equip him for essential collaboration with other specialists in allied fields.

This program should further be considered in two parts: (1) a program of education in Architecture and Planning to meet long-term needs, and (2) a short-term program to meet the immediacy of post-war reconstruction.

As a first step toward the realization of such a program, we respectfully suggest that the Secretary General of UNESCO appoint an interim chairman to whom detailed proposals may be addressed at the earliest time.

We further request that the reply to this letter be addressed on behalf of the signatories to: Dean Joseph Hudnut of Harvard University.

Signed:

Walter Baermann
Catherine Bauer
Martin L. Beck
Richard M. Bennett
John E. Burchard
Harold S. Buttenheim
Serge Chermayeff
Carlos Contreras
Le Corbusier
Thomas H. Creighton
Sigfried Giedion
Walter Gropius
George Howe
J. V. Hudnut
Henry A. Jandl
Roy Childs Jones
Henry L. Kamphoefner

George Fred Keck
Gyorgy Kepes
A. Lawrence Kocher
Ernest J. Kump
Jean Labatut
Liang Ssu-ch'éng
A. Gordon Lorimer
C. L. V. Meeks
Richard J. Neutra
Marcelo Roberto
Jose Luis Sert
Fred N. Severud
John K. Shear
G. E. Kidder Smith
Mies van der Rohe
Konrad Wachsmann

Dr. Huxley answered very encouragingly, appointing Dean Joseph Hudnut interim chairman. Six months later

CIAM took up the initiative (at its sixth congress held at Bridgwater, England, from September 7 to 14, 1947). An observer of the UNESCO followed the deliberations of the congress and reported to the Director General. Maxwell Fry, the well-known English architect, and I met Dr. Huxley and his staff in Paris and we agreed that CIAM would submit some preliminary remarks on architectural education at the Mexico Conference of UNESCO in November 1947.

As the remarks which I contributed on my own subject, history, are explanatory of my Princeton proposals, they may follow here.

PRELIMINARY REMARKS
ON ARCHITECTURAL EDUCATION

Addressed to the United Nations Educational, Scientific and Cultural Organization on behalf of Les Congres Internationaux d'Architecture Moderne by Sigfried Giedion.

The world-wide dissatisfaction with the present training of the architect compromises all the aspects of his education, from the abilities required to the qualifications and the degree of responsibility attained.

The main reason for this malaise is a one-sided *specialization*, one of the fundamental diseases of our time. Education in architecture, therefore, cannot be regarded as an isolated case, but must be integrated in the long run in the all-over reform of educational training.

In sharp contradiction to the present development, the most vital task of this period is to learn again how to *coordinate human activities*, for the creation of a coherent whole.

What we urgently need are people with coordinating minds, and it should therefore be one of the first purposes of education to promote in the young the development of this faculty. To achieve this, we must free ourselves of the departmentalized and encyclopedic conception of education and encourage instead the understanding and the comparing of the specific problems encountered and the methods evolved in the various domains of human thought and activity.

No single organization, no university, and no country is in a position to perform this task. UNESCO seems today the only agency in existence having the necessary means to accomplish this integration, which has to come about if our civilization is not to collapse.

In the field of architecture the situation may be described as follows:

In former periods a common pattern ran through the whole domain of architectural activity, uniting the crafts-man and the artist, the builder and the town planner. A common cultural background integrated almost unnotice-ably the various professions. The teamwork necessary to create a comprehensive whole could almost dispense with a conductor. The spirits were tuned together like the instruments of a string quartet.

All this has changed. The professions involved in archi-tectural activity acquire in their training a very limited outlook. The attempt is being made to turn the architect into a specialist in an ever-increasing number of continu-ously expanding disciplines, into a dilettantic mathemati-cian, engineer, statistician, art historian, sociologist, etc.

This hopeless undertaking must be abandoned, for a strictly *methodological* approach which will enable the student to know what questions he may ask and what solu-tions he may expect from other disciplines. He must be trained, of course, to become as skilled a craftsman as ever, but the stress must be laid today on his future role of a *coordinator*, so that he may be enabled to integrate the elements supplied by specialized knowledge into a *work of art*.

This involves in many respects a departure from present curricula and methods. As a historian, however, I shall limit myself to sketching the consequences of this concep-tion for the architect's study of history.

The architect's relation to history and to the past is

changing. In the nineteenth century the architecture of the ruling taste, and consequently the training of the architect, were concerned with shapes and forms. Students were trained to regard the past as a warehouse of forms, where one could borrow or pilfer *ad libitum*. Today a different attitude towards the past has evolved. Past, present, and future are regarded more and more as an indivisible whole. What we are looking for are the living forces and the spiritual attitudes which shaped the various periods, and most particularly we are interested in those problems of bygone civilizations which reveal a deep affinity with the present-day situation, just as modern painters and sculptors went back to so-called primitive cultures, to get support for the shaping of their own inner reality.

History conceived as an insight into the moving process of life comes closer and closer to the biological approach. We are interested today in knowing more than political, sociological, and economic occurrences. We want to know, in the manner of biologists, how the life of a culture took shape. This means exploring what one might call *anonymous history*. Methodological study of other periods will give the student a better insight into the specific nature of his own time, into its own accomplishments, and shortcomings in comparison to former civilizations.

The practical consequences in respect to the teaching of history, which still goes on as if nothing had happened since the middle of the last century, are that, instead of a history of styles and forms, a *typological* approach has to be introduced; instead of elaborating a false continuity from the Stone Age to the twentieth century, through an over-simplification and a purely formal description of various periods we must concentrate on the vertical lines going through history.

History teaching is ever tied to the fragment. But these fragments have to be chosen in such a way that new constellations will arise in the minds of the students. History can only be taught in this sense by people who have an intimate understanding of the architectural and the planning problems of the present, of their emotional as well as of their social aspects.

Closely related to this demand is the selection and limitation of subject matter in such a way that it can be tied up with the interests and the work of the student, as John Dewey has been proclaiming for the past half of a century. This, too, will help to eliminate nineteenth century methods based on a mechanistic piling up of unrelated facts, forgotten as quickly as they are acquired.

SECTION V
PLANNING

INTRODUCTION

BY THOMAS H. CREIGHTON

WITH this section the discussion leaves the somewhat theoretical field of the *bases for design* (social, physical, and intellectual) and approaches the problems faced in the *realization of design*. Here, in the next three sections, the procedure is from the great design problem to the small—from large-scale planning through the design of buildings to the consideration of individual objects.

It is probable that no designer would admit to thinking of a particular object—say, a chair—out of context with the room and the building in which it was going to be placed. Similarly, no architect would admit to thinking of a building design without considering the larger extensive environment of which that building would become a part. Yet it is true that in practice, because of limitations which he cannot control or because of his own limitations, many architects, as Theodore McCrosky expressed it before the Conference, "are inclined to think in terms of particular sites, and sometimes do not raise their eyes to see the site in relation to social, economic, and physical environment."

There is, then, the unfortunate distinction between the "planner" and the "architect." The Conference papers do little to bring the two closer together. Although everyone is willing to grant that the architect must "raise his eyes," there is no agreement that he is, or even should be, the planner of man's extended environment. Several appeals for teamwork were subscribed to without question, but the "architect-planner" whom Jose Luis Sert described at one point in the discussion as the inevitable coordinator of the team was considered by many to be no more important than any other player. Frederick J. Adams expressed the "planner's" attitude before he read his prepared statement:

My statement of position, which follows later, was prepared on the assumption that representative American architects, having in recent years become vitally interested in a field given by default for nearly half a century to engineers, landscape architects, and lawyers, wished to discuss in broad terms the responsibility of the architectural profession in the planning of communities, cities, and regions. . . .

After listening to the discussions which took place during the first four sessions of the Conference, I realized that I was suffering from an illusion when I prepared that statement. I should have known that we can count on the architects to remake the physical world, provided the public collaborates one hundred percent. Sert spoke of the need for "teams of experts" with the architect serving as coordinator of the team. We have been applying that idea for the past twelve years in our graduate city planning program at M.I.T., but occasionally it would be an engineer or social scientist who acted in the coordinating capacity. I realize now that this was a mistake, as architects, while frequently good coordinators, are rarely good collaborators.

Most participants felt that the division of opinion which could result in such a sarcastic comment from an able planner and educator comes to a large extent from a misunderstanding of the meaning of "architecture," a misunderstanding which the architects themselves are largely responsible for. It was recognized generally that broadscale planning as well as other aspects of the design of man's physical environment were lost to other professions "by default," as Adams said.

In his opening paper, Henry Churchill made an attempt to channel the discussion, which, if it had succeeded, might have brought a redefinition of physical "planning" in architectural terms. If physical planning is to have tangible meaning, he says, "we must bring it back to the third dimension in which people live and breathe." This third dimension, he points out, "is our special concern as architects."

But many of the planners, at least to this observer, seemed to continue to think of architecture as a matter of

THOMAS H. CREIGHTON

"visual aspects,"* and to think of the visual aspects in terms of prettiness or ugliness.

In this connection the conclusions of Section III are not carried over (except possibly by Talbot Hamlin) into the discussion that follows. Those conclusions seemed to include a belief that the esthetic reaction has a direct relation to human behavior and man's way of life. Yet the reader will find in Adams' paper a defense of the thesis that "ugly cities can be functionally well planned." To resolve this apparent conflict the Conference would have had to agree on one of three points: (1) an even clearer definition of "ugliness" than was arrived at in Section III, (2) a clear understanding of what a "functionally well planned" community is, or (3) an acceptance of the premise that planning a city is a very different process from planning a smaller environmental unit.

It was not the place of this section to discuss the first point. The second is the topic of several papers, but there is by no means agreement. Among the architects present, there was no willingness to agree to the last point. In prior correspondence, Carlos Contreras wrote:

All the relationships that may be established about *architectural* design and the social basis of *architecture* ... could be referred to (in this discussion) about *planning* design and the social basis of *planning*. Planning may be discussed as large-scale architecture.

So the misunderstanding between two branches of the same profession goes on, with this amelioration: there is a much clearer acceptance than in previous symposia of the two-part approach to planning, which includes both scientific analysis and three-dimensional expression.

Aside from the question of the nature of the planner, most of the discussion that follows has to do with the proc-

* In this connection it is interesting to note that a committee of the American Institute of Planners last year proposed the following as an official statement on education: ". . . it is well to state specifically that today's planner need have no outstanding genius or talent for 'design' in the esthetic, artistic, or engineering sense, though his planning education must provide him with some training and substantial perception in these fields."

· 129 ·

esses of planning *in a democracy*. The subject matter does not stray either into detailed discussion of techniques of city or regional planning (this was ruled out before the Conference; the closest approach to it is in Theodore McCrosky's paper) or into the more theoretical side-issues. Richard Neutra asked before the Conference, for instance, if there could not be an "inquiry into extra-planning or non-planning procedure in the past and present." He asked, "What actually is unplanned growth?" Perhaps such a discussion would have been interesting, but the answer seemed so obvious to so many people that it was implied rather than stated. One discussant after another points to our "blighted cities" as examples of unplanned growth and leaves it at that.

On the positive side, whether or not *planned* growth would include the building of large metropolises occupies a part of the discussion. Is the blight due to lack of planning, or is it inherent in the large city? Arthur Morgan made the strongest indictment of the city in his remark that "the architect working in an American city is building monuments in a graveyard." Recalling Roger Greeley's appeal (in Section I, page 13) to develop the possibility of the small town, Morgan points out that "America has never had a picture of what a small community might be." Theodore McCrosky, however, is sure of what it would be, or what its results would be, should it come to replace the "great cities" as "centers of civilization and culture." He says that he "forbears to contemplate a retrogression to a level of culture corresponding to the opportunities that could be offered to mankind in a civilization composed exclusively of small towns."

When the discussion turns, as it inevitably does, to the subject of *democratic* steps toward planning accomplishment, several important topics are discussed. There is the matter of the participation by the individual in planning schemes which seem too large for him to grasp; there is the matter of popular interest and support for the planner's result; there is the matter of the responsibility of the architect and planner in this process, of his part in the job which Walter Rolfe defines as "how to inspire humans through their own enterprise to want and to secure this new environment they might readily have."

Churchill approaches this subject in the first paper when he complains of the planning process "growing ever more tenuous, statistical, nebulous, and aimless," and asks that we do not "go too far toward Utopia." Talbot Hamlin reacted quickly to this and said that "planners must be Utopians, or revolutionists." Yet his reason was that "only by vivid presentation to the public of our Utopian plans can a popular demand for creative planning be created."

The need for support by the people affected is fully accepted, but the means of getting this support, and the means of stimulating the popular imagination and inspiring the popular understanding that will result in approval of the planning is not generally agreed upon. McCrosky points out that "the history of planning through the twentieth century bears out that plans have not been realized, for lack of organized popular understanding and support." Churchill points to one difficulty—that of getting individuals interested in planning for the common good—when he says that, although we must plan communities to "be lived in, worked in, played in by all kinds of people there are," we must remember that "in a complex and interacting world we cannot continue to live in an architecture created for the individual." (Ames, in his remarks from the point of view of esthetics, on page 87, would make an exception to this for the private single house.)

Churchill, then, calls for "coordination while preserving the essential dignity of the individual." Perhaps this is difficult to explain to the layman. Justement uses the word "cooperation," and believes that sufficiently bold plans will "stir the imagination" and result in the needed cooperation of all parties affected by the plan. To be thus bold, says Justement, the planner "will avoid details as he would the plague." He believes that the planner must "try to develop, to simplify, and to dramatize the principal features of the plan, so that they can be understood by the people."

Perhaps the most practical and specific suggestion for gaining democratic support, before as well as after the fact, is Roland Wank's reminder that "we are a pragmatic people, and believe what we see." From his experience he believes that "what the public sees, walks in, touches—that on which its judgment is based—is the site planning, the landscaping, and most of all the architecture." From this belief Wank evolves what he calls the "leap-frog" concept of planning progress—the physical accomplishments of one project acting as "testimony which will encourage" the next planning wave.

Despite its lack of conclusion, I believe that the Princeton Conference marks a point in the philosophy of planning when the architects are agreed that many sciences enter into the program for and affect the solution of extensive planning problems. I believe further that it marks a point when architects are beginning to realize that that interplay of scientific studies has danger of becoming the end, instead of the means of planning, and that they have the opportunity and the responsibility to carry planning on from this stage to full architectural accomplishment. There are many bold statements in the papers that follow pointing to the need for more than an economic study to improve the extensive environment of our present society and to cause that society to care about its improvement. In these pages the conception of planning begins to assume again that three-dimensional character which Churchill says it must have, if it "is not to lose all meaning." That in itself is an accomplishment.

THREE-DIMENSIONAL PLANNING

BY HENRY S. CHURCHILL

Architect and city planner, Henry Churchill has been consultant to the U.S. Housing Authority and to the New York

State Division of Housing. He is an active practitioner, partner in the firm of Churchill-Fulmer Associates, and has written a number of articles on planning and architecture, as well as the book, *The City Is The People* (1945).

In his paper below, Churchill makes a strong appeal for consideration of the "third dimension" in planning—a theme that is picked up again in several of the other papers.

I WOULD like, at the outset of this discussion on the extensive environment, to make a distinction that I feel is important, to distinguish between planning and building, between what often seems mostly wishful economic thinking and the creation of something in three dimensions. It has seemed to me, as I have watched the so-called planning process enlarge its scope from house to city and city to region and region to nation, growing ever more tenuous, statistical, nebulous, and aimless, that if physical planning is not to lose all meaning we must bring back to it the third dimension in which people live and breathe.

It is this extension into the third dimension that is our special concern as architects. Our arrangements of structures in space are limited by the uses to which land can be put. These land uses, in turn, are limited by law and custom. No matter what we plan, unless law and custom— the deep-seated *mores* of the people—are on our side, we cannot build those broad plans we put on paper.

I hope, therefore, that we may here talk about planning in such a way that three-dimensional reality, architecture that is, runs through the discussion like a theme. We can perhaps also safely digress into the fourth dimension of time, whose beginning is the sprouting seed, whose essence is the rhythm of the revolving world, and whose end may be not the scattering of the atom but the dissolution of the human brain.

On the other hand I trust we will not drift off into the futility of economics. As architects, as thinkers, as human beings, we must probe deeper into the meaning of our theme. It is our job, or at least a part of it, to give such validity to our ideas and such vitality to our concepts that their realization becomes a necessity for our economic survival.

Nor do I think that it is of much importance, here, whether we have this, that, or the other kind of implementing legislation. What we should try to do is to clarify what kind of city, what sort of environment, we would build for ourselves and the few people we know and the millions we don't know, if we had our way and could find understanding of their way. We must always remember that this city we wish to create must be lived in, worked in, played in by all the kinds of people there are. If we do so we will not, I am sure, go too far towards Utopia—which was, I believe, a mirror of dictatorship.

And yet, in a complex and highly interacting world we cannot continue to live in an architecture created for the individual regardless of his basic interdependence. It is the creation, consciously and architecturally, of an extensive environment which will use the techniques of coordination while preserving the essential dignity of the individual that should, I think, be the subject of our dreams.

THE VALUE OF UTOPIAS

BY TALBOT HAMLIN

Architectural historian and critic, Talbot Hamlin has been an influential teacher in the School of Architecture at Columbia University, as well as Avery Librarian at that institution. His several books have been important additions to architectural literature; they include *The Enjoyment of Architecture* (Charles Scribner's Sons, 1926), *Architecture Through the Ages* (G. P. Putnam's Sons, 1940), *Greek Revival Architecture in the United States* (Oxford University Press, 1944) and the comprehensive work entitled *Forms and Functions of Twentieth Century Architecture*, which he has edited for the Columbia University Press.

THE experience of countless city-plan commissions, planners, and housing authorities reveals the discouraging fact that, under the present economic and political system, any discussion of large-scale replanning is largely academic. So long as profits control the problem of land usage, no major replanning achievements seem to be possible. Planners by their very nature, therefore, must be either Utopian or revolutionary. Utopianism or revolution seem inevitable ways of thinking; there is no possible middle way, save tinkering to preserve a little longer the confusions of the present by making them slightly less intolerable. Moreover, Utopian study may be of the greatest value, because only by studying Utopian schemes can the real possibilities which our technical advance makes possible be discovered, for only by Utopian methods can these advantages be made available to all the people. And only large and daring plans have the power to fire public enthusiasm. Hence it is only by the most vivid and graphic presentation to the public of Utopian plans that a vital popular demand for creative planning can be aroused.

TEAMWORK IN PLANNING

BY FREDERICK J. ADAMS

Head of the Department of City and Regional Planning in the School of Architecture and Planning at the Massachusetts Institute of Technology, Mr. Adams has not been content with academic considerations of planning. He has been consultant to many planning bodies, state and municipal, and since 1943 he has been Chairman of the City Planning Commission of Cambridge, Massachusetts. He is also President of the American Institute of Planners; a member of the governing boards of the American Society of Planning Officials and the National Council on Community Improvement; and Vice-Chairman of the Committee on the Hygiene of Housing of the American Public Health Association.

Adams' paper may displease many architects; it may also

make some of them wonder whether they have either missed opportunities or misjudged their capabilities.

IT MIGHT have been more appropriate if the agenda for this discussion had given greatest emphasis to those elements of the extensive environment which are predominantly visual in character. In that way we might have reached conclusions on some of the aspects of environmental planning of particular interest to this group. Regional planning is primarily a social and political science, no more closely identified with architecture than it is with engineering, economics, or law, and I do not see how, in the two hours at our disposal, we can expect to achieve any constructive results if we give the economic and political aspects the emphasis they deserve. However, as these topics are listed in the agenda, I need not apologize for bringing them in.*

I do not entirely agree with the assumption stated in the program that "overall planning without consideration of detail is as academic as detail planning without the consideration of the whole of which it is a part." Fundamental problems of planning of the extensive environment are not primarily visual ones, at least in the early stages of the planning process. Visual aspects are limited to the range of vision, which usually does not incorporate a whole neighborhood, much less a city or region. Among the basic problems in regional planning are the determination of policies on location of industry, population density, conservation of natural resources, economics of land use, and so forth. The primary objective in planning at the regional level is a synthesis of the social, economic, and physical aspects, and their relative importance in specific cases is largely a matter of timing. Little progress will be made if we continue to think of comprehensive planning as primarily an architectural or engineering problem.

* A set of "axioms and assumptions" was handed the participants prior to the Conference sessions. Since few discussants paid them the attention Mr. Adams did, they have not been included here.—Ed.

FREDERICK J. ADAMS

Cities should be attractive to the eye as well as the mind—there need be no conflict between beauty and economy or efficiency—but ugly cities can be functionally well planned, and it is possible for a city or region to be esthetically satisfying and yet violate fundamental planning criteria. A bridge, a school, or a large-scale housing project may be structurally sound and architecturally attractive; but if the bridge or school is in the wrong place or if the housing project commands higher rents than the people can pay, it is bad planning although perhaps not bad design in the visual sense.* A one-industry town or a one-class suburb may be socially or economically undesirable. Does it follow that it is esthetically bad? Which is the more important? However, while most of the problems in planning are not predominantly structural or visual, they undoubtedly require creative imagination and an ability to think in terms of broad perspective. For this reason an architectural training has advantages over a narrow type of engineering training in developing future planning technicians.

Planning in a democracy involves effective citizen participation. The planner is only one of many technicians. Broadly speaking, he is no more important than members of a planning commission or city council, or the head of a line department. A comprehensive plan is not the creation of a master mind but is essentially a collaborative effort. The social and economic ideas of a community or region should be expressed in the physical pattern, not the pet ideas of the technician. City or regional plans lose by being identified too much with an individual planner; the latter

* Questioned about the apparent inconsistency between this point of view and Adelbert Ames's conclusions (page 82) Adams wrote later: "Ames's experiments were concerned with psychological reactions to visual experience. Where the eye can comprehend the whole of an object, I can agree with his statement about the relation of esthetics to function. The physical organization of a city or a region cannot be comprehended as a visual 'whole,' and its social or economic organization even less so. If the bank of a river were developed for (a) industrial purposes, (b) residential purposes, (c) recreational purposes, (d) flood control purposes, [could] the eye detect which treatment best satisfies the social and economic requirements?"—Ed.

· 137 ·

should consider himself as an interpreter rather than a dictator.

To achieve success in comprehensive planning, initiative and leadership on the part of state and local governments is essential. If we are to make real progress in this country, a change in the attitude of the average American citizen to government enterprise must take place, and the planning process must be interwoven into the fabrics of government at all levels. Only by wide public understanding of planning objectives and joint action by all parties concerned can we hope to bring about the desired changes in the overall environment. This is no less true of the esthetic and psychological aspects of the environment than it is of the economic or institutional aspects.

What is needed is teamwork—teamwork between and within professional groups and between such groups and the public at large. The architect has as important a part to play as has any technician in the development of our communities and regions into better places to live, work, and play. He frequently can and should provide the leadership. But let's recognize that both teamwork and leadership are essential and that there is so much work to be done that we cannot afford to spend our energies in arguing questions of protocol.

URBAN REPLANNING

BY THEODORE T. MCCROSKY

Mr. McCrosky, executive director of the Greater Boston Development Committee, contributed a paper in Section II on Administrative Limitations in planning. Here he adds to the discussion of planning itself an acute analysis of the specific problems facing the planner who concerns himself with that most pressing of needs—the replanning of urban areas.

THE growth of metropolitan areas may be likened to the spreading of a pool of heavy molasses as it is poured rapidly from a can. For a while, the center of the pool gets thicker and thicker and the spread is slow. Then, as the can is emptied, the molasses continues to spread over a wider and wider area and thins out at the center.

The basic problems facing the city and the region are intrinsically related. They vary little from region to region throughout the country. They differ only in severity and priority of importance. The underlying factors are in all cases (a) congestion, (b) obsolescence, and (c) unguided development. There is another factor, or more properly a limiting condition, which seriously affects the financial ability of local governments to solve their problems adequately. This is the slowing-up of the long-time trends of increasing population, increasing taxable values and increasing tax revenues. Cities and, to a less extent, metropolitan areas are approaching stability of population, and in some cases have already passed their peak and begun to decline. They are faced with the urgent need for physical improvements but are drastically limited in their capacity to pay for them. This situation affects all planning problems and solutions, but is essentially a problem of government structure and financial resources.

In terms of the needs and desires of the people, the four most vital functions that they expect their city to provide for them are: a place to live; a place to work; recreational facilities, outdoor and indoor; and means of transportation connecting home, work, and recreation.

Our cities are wearing out. People have moved out into the suburbs because better living conditions were thus achievable, and because improved transportation made such moves feasible, even though often inconvenient. The shift of industry is motivated by more complicated factors, but better operational conditions and transportational feasibility of outlying locations are again the ruling forces.

It is recognized that when the old areas of our cities are rebuilt population densities should be lower than existing structures provide. Thus, a certain degree of draining out of families to the suburbs is manifestly desirable. However, eventual *balance* must be achieved between the suburban trend and the attracting power of the central city. We cannot plan for chaos, nor for the abandoning of all that our great cities mean as centers of civilization and culture. The writer forbears to contemplate a retrogression to a level of culture corresponding to the opportunities that could be offered to mankind in a civilization composed exclusively of small towns.

In order to assure the attracting power of large cities, the following principles would appear to be basic in the consideration of problems of redesign and rebuilding:

1. Creation of home and apartment neighborhoods, largely self-contained, with most of the advantages of the best suburban developments, plus greater accessibility to places of work. Play lots, schools, playgrounds, athletic fields, community centers, clinics, and shopping facilities should be built into the neighborhood design. Smoke control is a factor in achieving urban neighborhood amenity. Utilization of the superblock principle can reduce excessive street area and secure protection from vehicular traffic.

2. Creation of office building and downtown shopping districts that will be not merely "modern," but "ahead of their times." Well-spaced high buildings, connected by two-story retail stores, appear more advantageous than a lower but uniform height for all structures. Roofs of the low buildings should be treated as parks. Ample off-street parking and off-street loading space for trucks is essential. Rebuilding operations should normally embrace an absolute minimum of one city block.

3. Creation of integrated districts for small manufacturing companies, carefully located and provided with modern transportation and employee welfare

services on a pooled basis for all participating industries.

4. Provision of transit and traffic facilities, based on the principle that public carriers and private automobiles are complementary rather than competitive. No subway congestion was ever solved by building a highway; and no traffic jam was ever solved by building a subway. As commerce is the lifeblood of the city, express highway facilities into and out of the urban center should be open to trucks and busses. The place for the restricted pleasure parkway is on the urban periphery or beyond. Principal residential and work centers must be interconnected by both rapid transit and grade-separated highways. Attention must be paid to the provision of circumferential as well as radial connections. Subcenters can be stimulated by planning the junctions of radials and circumferentials.

5. Provision of circumferential or greenbelt parks; and of radial sector parks between radial transit lines. These two types of park belts should serve as buffers between noncompatible land uses.

6. Pooling of private financial resources, on a large scale, to achieve integrated rebuilding operations both residential and non-residential.*

* Another aspect of pooling of private interests was suggested by Arthur Holden in a letter written to participants in this section before the Conference. Speaking of the need for inter-relationships among adjacent privately owned buildings, Holden wrote: "Where the relations of various buildings are concerned, we are just beginning to recognize that zoning ordinances written to control setbacks on the individual lot and expressed in terms of bulk and area fall far short of working out an appropriate regulation of group design. Indeed, requirements of the type that we have now often militate against good group design. . . . For example, it doesn't injure certain blocks in the older section of the city to put high buildings at the end, provided it is done in a way that does not overshadow or destroy values. Yet, a high building invading the center of the open space in the middle of the block might, in many cases, be definitely detrimental. On the other hand, if done on a large scale where groups of blocks are planned together, such as in Rockefeller Center, high buildings can be planned in the center of the block and the buildings so grouped that adequate light

7. Coordinated utilization of federal, state, regional, and local public funds to carry out the public features of the plan.

8. Continuous stimulation of the public appetite for the fruits of city rebuilding. Every citizen must be shown in what ways he personally will benefit.

HISTORICAL VALUES:
THE FORGOTTEN CRITERION

BY TALBOT HAMLIN

For a second time Talbot Hamlin enters the discussion on planning. As a historian, he makes a plea for one more principle in urban planning beyond those Theodore McCrosky listed.

ANY existing community is a living thing. It possesses a present to be analyzed and a future which may be planned, but in most cases it also possesses a past. This past affects not only the forms of the community but also the attitude of its population, for a community with a rich past has emotional values which nothing else can replace.

These values are expressed in buildings, street arrangements, and groups of buildings—as, for instance, in the case of the Vieux Carré of New Orleans or the streets of Beacon

---

and air may be provided between the buildings. Thus it is clear that where large areas are well planned, the execution of construction in accordance with such a plan is a far better protection than specific prohibitions against individual lot development. This would have to be accomplished by covenants entered into by individual property owners which would allow for the execution of a large-scale plan on a group basis. Principles should be explored for making equitable adjustments between the properties which participate in such a plan, such as the payment of a rent for air rights or the sharing of a portion of income gained by reason of the execution of a group plan. We will need to think about methods for adjusting the tax base and the methods of tax collection which will recognize the contributions made by various property owners to the execution of a group plan."
—Ed.

Hill in Boston—and the existence of these expressions of the past is one of the reasons why people love and admire certain communities or go to visit them and study them. Frequently the attitude of a population toward its community is also deeply and vitally affected by the preservation of such monuments. People care for what they love, and they tend to love shapes and forms and colors which their predecessors have created and which have come to be integral parts of their own background.

The modern city planner frequently seems blind to any such considerations. To him a beautiful area, seen only in its economic aspects, may appear as a blighted area, and he is all for its complete destruction and reconstruction. But the true planner, it seems to me, must consider the total life of the community and, in order to guide its future intelligently, must take advantage of all existing points of beauty or historical monuments as essential elements in the scheme he is planning. Thus one of the surveys which should precede any planning operation in connection with an existing community should be a survey to discover and spot historical monuments and structures or groups of structures of outstanding architectural or expressive beauty or historical value.

The attracting power of any community comes largely from the fact that in it are expressed the fruits of a long, gradual historical development; past, present, and future interpenetrate each other—it is that which makes the city seem alive. Is it not then the planner's duty to attempt to incorporate into the new just as much of the old as is visually attractive and can be made somehow usable? It is this approach which has distinguished the resurrection of the Vieux Carré in New Orleans, once a blighted area and, by all city planning standards, worthy of nothing but destruction and replacement. It is the same attempt to preserve the best of the old and to integrate it with the new which has distinguished Robert Mills Houses, a USHA housing development in Charleston, South Carolina. It thus seems that the preservation of what is in itself beautiful, historically expressive, and well liked is one of the means by which city planners can produce a living community and not a sterile diagram.

DECENTRALIZATION

BY ARTHUR E. MORGAN

Dr. Morgan, who contributed a major paper to Section I, here steps into the discussion on large-scale planning with a sharp divergence from McCrosky's point of view. Instead of replanning our large cities, he says, we should begin planning a decentralized society.

THE architect working in an American city is building monuments in a graveyard. The American city today draws to itself the cream of the population of all America, and then extinguishes the family lines of those it attracts. City families on the average die out in four generations or less. If our large cities were not recruited from small communities, in four generations they would shrink to perhaps a quarter of their present populations.

America never has had a picture of what a small community might be. Until such a vision does emerge there will continue to be an exodus to the city and an impoverishment of our small communities, which are the source of our future population. The small community must supply all the basic needs of good living—an adequate economic basis, hygienic environment, education, culture, recreation, and especially opportunity for pioneering and adventure. The architect should be turning his mind to this need, and should be helping the emergence of a vision of the great community.

Radical as the step seems, American industry and culture should decentralize, leaving in the city only the functions and population actually needed there. Then urban squalor and small town deadness would largely disappear, and both city and country might thrive and be wholesome. The suburb is not the answer. Wholesome decentralization calls for many leaders, including architects, but such leadership would largely sacrifice the prospect of large present financial income. Is it therefore impracticable?

PLANNING AND THE INDIVIDUAL

BY LOUIS JUSTEMENT

Mr. Justement, Fellow in the American Institute of Architects and Chairman of that body's Committee on Urban Planning, is an architect and planner who has practiced in Washington, D.C., since 1919. He is author of the book, *New Cities for Old* (McGraw-Hill, 1946).

Mr. Justement here brings the discussion to the matter of the part the individual in the community must play in the planning process, and the professional's relation to this problem in democratic action.

ONE might have supposed that a Conference on Planning Man's Physical Environment would have consisted, to a large extent, in discussing various planning and design techniques—a supposition which would appear all the more valid because, in this instance, the conferees were almost all architects and planners. Technical aspects of planning and design, however, constituted a relatively small part of the discussion. I believe that this is both significant and encouraging.

It is significant because it is an indication that, as planners and architects, we can no longer perform our functions adequately on the basis of executing, as technicians, projects conceived by others. We must assume our share of responsibility, as citizens, in forming and developing public opinion. For the essence of planning is forethought—the conscious striving to reach a goal. Our first task, therefore, is to aid in defining our social objectives. What is it that we want? If we can secure agreement concerning our goal, it should not be too difficult to devise methods of reaching it.

It is encouraging that architects should participate in this search for valid social objectives, because, through the effort to define these objectives, they may succeed, incidentally, in reaching another goal: the development of a contemporary style of architecture that is as fitting to our civilization as the great styles of the past were to past civilizations.

How can we, as architects and planners, perform our function as leaders of public opinion? I believe that our plans must be sufficiently bold to stir the imagination of others and to create in them the desire to collaborate. An able city planner will avoid details as he would the plague, except to the extent that an understanding of the details enables him to develop an adequate comprehensive plan. He must try to develop, to simplify, and to dramatize the principal features of the plan so that they can be understood by the people. But those who understand will, in many cases, want to help in the development as well as in the realization of the plan. This is a desire that should not be frustrated; it should, on the contrary, be stimulated. For the city must be something more than the materialization of a good plan imposed on a docile community by a clever planner. The city we are attempting to build—or to rebuild—should result from the conscious striving of an entire community.

We should devise a planning procedure that facilitates large-scale planning for those features—and only those features—that require a unified approach. Simultaneously, however, we should permit and encourage decentralized planning and a maximum variety of solutions wherever variety is permissible. It is time that we, as planners, should learn to plan our work so that it will stimulate the creative ability of the individual where this is possible and yet stimulate the spirit of cooperation and collaboration where this is necessary. The gregarious and yet individualistic modern man will not be happy if one-half of his nature is thwarted for the benefit of the other.

WALTER T. ROLFE

CREATING A DESIRE FOR PLANNING

BY WALTER T. ROLFE

Mr. Rolfe, architect from Houston, Texas, cuts straight to the heart of the question of *democratic* planning. Going beyond the usual question of how public support for planned projects can be achieved, he asks how the basic *desire* for a better environment, which will inspire those planning schemes in the first instance, can be stimulated.

A MINOR theme of frustration has occasionally appeared in the discussion up to this point. It is important, because it may indicate that man himself must help the professionally talented to extend human environment beyond all present margins of human experience or imagination. Perhaps this frustration is clear impatience with present environmental failures; it is expressed so honestly by professionals who have lived and worked close to uncloistered life—close to those who often do not visualize man's physical environment in terms of society as a whole, but only in terms of money, personal gain, and extortionate profit. Great creative thinking in the presence of uninspirable people often opens an extensive gulf, and results in apparent frustration.

The varied experiences of these highly talented professional people, engaged in creating a better human environment, indicate the final difficulty of planning for those who may not wish it, do not understand it, or simply will not have it. What a deep and often uncrossable gulf lies between philosophical, idealistic (sometimes called communistic) planning, and the more earthy, slow, and perhaps more workable process of planning that arises from human needs, desires, and resources. Planning ought to come from within, but of its own power it seldom does. The basic problem, then, is how to inspire humans through their own free enterprise to want and to secure this new environment they might readily have. How may they have it—and yet be able to pay for it?

Successful planning from above is on the records. TVA is well known. However, it seems more important to a whole people that they be educated to *demand* a planning program, in which they have a more personal and intimate part, continuing and creative. We appreciate an environment all the more if we have had a part in the creation of it. Things done *for* us are often resented, because of the implied lack of talent in our not having thought of them before they were done for us.

The democratic way is the slow way, but the solid and permanent one. The desirability and practicality of a finer physical environment must become part of our thinking about our whole way of life before it can become a reality. It is not enough to train our thinkers and our creative people—architects, planners, sociologists, and all the others required to create the inspirational environment. It is equally important to develop in the hearts of all human beings the desire for this environment, with full knowledge and understanding of what it will do for them and to them. Then we must create the wealth to pay for this better environment for the common good of our whole nation.

Physical environment, however, is not enough. It is a sort of end product of the spiritual hunger that makes nations sing because they cannot help it. In the very soul of man is a strong desire and a hunger that sends his mind into the universe, that frees him from intellectual slavery. This poetic urge is manifest in his history, his aspirations, his literature, and his other creative works. It is even manifest in his most secret frustrations.

He may not like his failure cities and his crime-producing environment any better than the planners do. The planners know that they could be made better. The techniques for proper planning exist, and the concepts of improved environment have been developed—professionally. But the people who are going to *use* the new environment must also believe in the new concepts. It all comes back to people and their own conceptions of the kind of place human beings desire to call their own.

Our thinking must start with them and end with them. Planning an adequate environment is no more abstract an ideal than any found in the basic tenets of democracy, but we must first think through an educational program that inculcates it, and then work at it just as zealously as we do any other aspect of democracy. It must be woven through and through the basic culture of civilization if we are ever to have it. First we must visualize it, then we must all desire it enough to create the instruments by which it may be accomplished.

Man has a long way to go before the environment he creates will have anything of the sweep, the spiritual inspiration, the magnificent scale that are everywhere around him in the environment he did not create, often does not see, and seldom understands. Only by thinking and working hard will he be able to make much of an impression on the cosmos that scarcely tolerates him or knows or cares that he is often an inharmonious and ungrateful critter at best, yet capable of projecting his intellectual powers beyond the stars.

DEMOCRATIC PLANNING

BY ROLAND A. WANK

Mr. Wank was Chief Architect for the Tennessee Valley Authority during the period of greatest planning and construction activity in that region, and remains its Chief Consulting Architect. He is now associated with the architectural firm of Fellheimer and Wagner in New York. His paper, which is an extension of extemporaneous remarks made from the floor at the Conference, sums up beautifully the problems which the other participants have raised of planning in a democracy—the slowness, the inevitable opposition, the value of completed though imperfect work, and finally the faith and devotion necessary to carry through to the "three-dimensional reality" which was the aim established in the beginning of this section.

MUCH has been said in this discussion about the kind of physical environment to plan for; little about how it is

149

done. Yet the two are obviously pertinent to each other; there is not much satisfaction in planning things that have no prospect of being carried out.

The writer's attention has been turned to planning by a process which must be fairly typical of the experiences of other architects. During years of preparation he learned what buildings should be like; as he worked on projects for actual clients, there were few opportunities to carry out more than a scattering fraction of the notions instilled in him. It seemed that some overall limitations always got in the way—sometimes it was land, at other times financing, building codes, or labor unions. One gradually comes to the conclusion that before good buildings can be put up as a matter of course rather than exception something needs to be done about the conditions surrounding all the business of building. And it is obvious that even minor changes in such conditions require coordinated, planned, and sustained campaigns.

To predict what kind of plan and how much of it has a chance of success is essentially a political judgment. To possess that kind of judgment and still persevere in planning requires a religious faith in democracy, and unlimited patience. All democratic planning is slow, but it seems particularly halting and discontinuous in our country. Latins, Scandinavians, Swiss seem to be less inhibited by emphasis on property rights, especially on the sanctity of land ownership—and the difference is evident in the physical appearance of their cities, forests, and farms. Their publicly owned enterprises—which furnish some fixed points and continuity to physical planning—cover large portions of their national economies. Even Britain, where most of our property notions originate, has gone a long way in that direction—under the spur of post-war necessity, to be sure.

By way of contrast, American planning seems to be palliative rather than creative. In the semantic scale, planning is one of the "bad" words, only a few steps this side of dictatorship. Most of it is done to ameliorate conditions that have become unendurable, follows the line of least resistance rather than logic, and is enthusiastically thrown overboard when the emergency has passed.

To illustrate: Perhaps the most significant and certainly the popularly best understood planning—our own contribution to the world planning movement—pertains to highways, to cope with the permanent emergency of automobile traffic which is also our own peculiar contribution. New and more magnificent roads are built after the old ones have been intolerably crowded for years because that is the line of least resistance rather than an attack on fundamental causes. When the new ones become equally crowded, still others will be built, at staggering costs of cash, public debt, and land area occupied. In the meantime parking, which always collides with more valuable property rights, goes from worse to the impossible much faster than any measures yet proposed could possibly ameliorate it, even if they were enacted. In the suburban business centers, conditions begin to approximate the downtown metropolis as more of the parking lots between stores are built upon to house more businesses to trade more with a public that is less and less able to reach them.

That is the record in a matter which touches every citizen in one of his most sensitive spots—his automobile. In matters about which he thinks less intensely, the record is worse. As said before, such planning as we can boast of is accomplished when things have become intolerable, and therefore primarily during depressions. We establish the TVA, for example, when poverty in the South has reached bankruptcy coincidentally with a crying need of other sections for more solvent customers. Five years later the low point has been passed, and a bill for more TVA's goes down to defeat in Congress. Federal public housing is set up when unemployment in the building trades turns attention to shameful slum conditions, and is cheerfully hobbled in the post-war period of high employment, though housing is scarcer than ever. Nothing is quite as detrimental to planning progress as a period of prosperity.

The opposition to planning includes people of many

different motives—some sincere, some not. The most effective cry is to link planning with dictatorship—therefore, the absence of planning with democracy.

This is serious business, both for planning and for democracy, because it is doubtful whether the latter can survive without assimilating into itself a much greater measure of the former. To bring this assimilation about while there is still time is the greatest task of planners and of architects, greater than any individual plan, building, interior, or furnishings item. Yet all those have a critical significance in the process. To understand that significance, the writer would like to present what might be called the "leap-frog" concept of planning progress.

One of the indictments against planning on any comprehensive scale is that, even if it were popularly acceptable, there just aren't enough people with know-how to carry it on. All too often, the indictment is true; for how could the know-how be acquired except by previous experience?

Every bit of accomplished plan, therefore, is thrice valuable. Once, for what it accomplished; twice, for what it added to planning experience; thrice, for what public evidence it presents for the case of planning.

It is on this point of evidence that architecture is vital. Good architecture, of course, follows the planning that created the basic conditions for it. Yet it also precedes the next planning wave, leap-frog fashion, by presenting testimony which will encourage public support.

The nature of planning measures is rather abstruse. It may be some financial program, or some law full of whereases, understandable only to experts, that is ultimately responsible for a waterfront park, a housing project, or a dam across a valley. But we are a pragmatic people, and are impressed only by what we see.

Also, like humans everywhere, we have infinite capacity for adjustment; we make out as best we can under the conditions that be and come to take them for granted, no matter how unnecessarily aggravating they are; having made the adjustments, we even prefer known hardship to unfamiliar relief, until we have been shocked out of the mood by repeated and striking demonstrations.

Opinion may differ about the professional merit of the particular projects I should like to cite as examples. But taking them at the popular estimate of their worth, I believe it is safe to say that Rockefeller Center did more for public understanding and support of large-scale redevelopment than the best textbooks; that the Norris and Greenbelt villages had the same effect on integrated community planning; Jones Beach made the desire for public recreation parks nation-wide.

Each project leaves, upon its conclusion, more experienced planners; each adds to the base on which public support for further planning can be solicited. There was a time, not long ago, when of *before and after* illustrations for texts on planning only the *before* photographs were domestic; views of the *after* had to be borrowed from foreign sources and were, accordingly, much less convincing. Similarly citizen groups, boards of directors and legislators could be taken on tours to see horrible conditions with their own eyes, but the improvements to be attained had to be imagined.

The Great Depression, the New Deal, and the war left in their wake a modest initial stock of positive accomplishment, of which the intrinsic worth, great as it may be, becomes almost insignificant by comparison to the promotional value.

To revert to the service of the architect: the site planning, the landscaping, and, most of all, the architecture are what the public sees, walks in, touches—on that its judgment is perforce based. If those are approved, the approval reflects upon the planning; if not, planning progress suffers. The architect (and his associates, the site and landscape designers) is, in a manner of speaking, the retail purveyor of the ultimate consumers' goods. If his wares don't sell, the producers and, back of them, the capital-goods industries are helpless.

And this service to a long-enduring cause is often the

principal satisfaction the architect can expect from practice in this imperfect world. With few exceptions, each project falls far short of what the architect knows it should be; progress from one decade to another is heartbreakingly slow; most of us know that we will die without having done our best. But each crop of projects is like a wave of shock troops, to form a bridge for the next.

This is the only way the planning concept progresses in a democracy, and it is certainly preferable to the dreary alternative of dictatorship. The great question—perhaps the supreme question of history—is how to make the process fast enough. I suppose the same question arises in other areas of human affairs; but speaking of physical planning, can its progress be made faster than the continued deterioration and destruction of the heritage we now possess? Are we running fast enough now at least to stay in one place?

Whether one answers this affirmatively or negatively in his innermost heart is perhaps the clearest test of one's faith in the ultimate victory of democracy.

SECTION VI

SPACE USE

INTRODUCTION

BY THOMAS H. CREIGHTON

T HE original full title of this session of the Conference was "The Building as the Limiting Element of Space." Since the discussion could be applied to groups of buildings or even communities of buildings, and since most of the argument had to do not with space limitations but rather space conception, that first title no longer seems descriptive.

The "practical" architect need not expect here a description in detail of how to plan a hospital or a school or shopping center. That was not the purpose of the gathering at Princeton. The papers are still general in content, philosophical in concept. However, for that truly practical person who is concerned with what makes the proper design of our physical environment today different from what was the proper design of man's environment in other times, the discussion now comes down to real cases. A better understanding of the nature of space and man's relation to it due to physical, physiological, and psychological studies which have been made, and an appreciation of the modern concepts of time and space, springing from recent philosophical, mathematical, and other scientific inquiries actually constitute the most immediate and practical design progress.

In his paper in Section II John Burchard, searching for the distinguishing characteristic of architecture in our time, said, "The great distinction of today is that we ask that more classes of people be served by our buildings; we demand for every building a degree of specialization hitherto unknown." Burchard was thinking in terms of the technical requirements of buildings. In this section the discussants are rather thinking in terms of the larger design concepts. Which is more valuable? So that the question can be better answered, I would like to quote from a letter of Burchard's in which he went further into the "special

· 157 ·

requirements of our time" than he did in the prepared paper referred to. He said:

The great social demands of today for hospitals, schools, housing groups, transportation terminals, distribution and recreational centers, power complexes (TVA), are the spur to whatever is in the long run to be significant in our architecture. Whether the office building was ever a comparable spur in an earlier day is debatable; but surely the church and the hospice were in the Middle Ages; the theater, the temple, and the agora in classic time.

Another participant commenting on the program, before the Conference itself, also wished that this particular section might concern itself with the matter of contemporary *demands* on buildings. He wrote:

I feel that there should be some consideration at this point of the various social uses for buildings today. The physical building itself is a limiting unit, but specific space uses within the building are further delimiting. The attempt on the part of some designers to make structures act for various or alternating social purposes is an attempt to alleviate some of the limitations and gain greater design freedom. Modular planning is another expression of desire for less limitation by the unit structure.

Henry Churchill replied to that commentary in words that come back fairly closely to Burchard's point that the important thing about buildings today is their specific technical social use. He wrote:

I have a feeling that the achievement of no limitation, i.e., *complete* flexibility, results only in a meaningless abstraction of form. When the world was "without form and void," there were no limitations, and form appeared only when the Creator set the land aside from the water and gave shape and meaning to things. A use, an objective, is the primary need for the elimination of chaos, and it seems to me that what needs to be discussed, in a philosophy of architecture, is the rationale of limitations;

what elements of use, material, and spirit are conducive
to the creation of a great work of art. Modular architecture is not a removal of limitations but a freeing of technique, a release of power to be applied not to the stultifying task of *how* to do it but to the spiritual one of *what*
to do within the limitations of purpose.

Despite these various appeals toward a discussion of what
to do with our buildings, the papers deal with the broadest
possible questions of how to control, delimit, enclose, or
free the part of space which composes an individual architectural design. I believe that the decision of the discussants
to speak in these larger design terms was a wise one. While
there would probably be little argument among the people
represented in this book that the ultimate social use of
structures is the most important criterion in judging the
planning of man's self-made environment in any period of
history, once that fact has been stated there is little more to
say on the subject without going into a technical discussion
which is not the purpose of this symposium. There are
books and standards and studies under way and completed
and contemplated on the subjects of hospital planning and
school planning and store planning. Admirable papers
have been written on program development and the isola-
tion, for full study in their settings, of social planning problems. Architects generally are aware of these available data.
Yet the fact remains that architects generally today are not
producing buildings which are fully useful social instruments for our time. As George Howe points out in his
paper, the very new buildings arising on the Princeton
grounds while the discussions were going on failed, despite
careful technical use studies, to produce significant form.

So this section of the Conference discussion attempts to
discover the basic attitudes toward space use that might allow full realization of the technical social purpose for
buildings of our time. Comments that George Fred Keck
made before the meeting begin to point to the subject matter that was chosen. He wrote:

Inventions affect building design; the newer sciences of

sociology and psychology affect the planning of buildings. Newer developments in transportation, such as the
automobile and airplane, affect design and planning.
The façade becomes of less importance. Human beings
like crowding; they also like the wide open spaces. They
can now have both. Buildings must be designed and
planned for the climate into which they are placed, and
must be a function of the natural phenomena surrounding them . . . this premise will develop regional types of
buildings over our country. Space itself is used as a design element.

To Keck, then, the "newer sciences" and the new attitude toward the use of space are the important things. But
the best answer to our original question—which is more
important to basic design, specific social use or the manner
of space use—is perhaps contained in George Howe's original commentary on the program, very little of which found
its way into the paper that he ultimately read. It is, however, an excellent introduction to those final remarks, as it
emphasizes the importance of the creation of "significant
space" as against stated requirements—the specific program. Howe wrote:

In the thrifty 30's I once asked a real estate agent what
were his requirements for an office building. He answered, "I want a monumental exterior and a lot of small
offices inside."

So crassly stated the program sounds absurd enough.
After a moment's reflection, however, one cannot but
recognize that this is the formula still generally adopted
for office buildings, from the porticoed palaces of Washington to the aspiringly vertical towers of New York.

Mild disapproval of this sort of spatial deception was
voiced by a Washington observer. Issuing from the end-
less corridors of a government office building recently
built, he was asked by a friend what he thought of it. "It
seems to me," he answered, looking back at its colossal
columns, "there is much less here than meets the eye."

Much less of what? Much less significant space, one may

presume, than the scale and weight of the limiting building would indicate. In any building worthy of the name
of a work of art, the observer seems to imply, there should
be a correspondence between the visible structure and
the significance of the space it limits.

In the first flowerings of the art of building, as in ancient Greece for the classical culture, let us say, or in
medieval Europe for our western culture, this correspondence is plain to see and has been extensively commented on. In simple societies living space, working
space, fighting space, and worshipping space flowered
into their limiting building forms effortlessly and more
or less spontaneously. The instinctive expression of symbolic space in religious edifices, which seemed to be one
with the collective unconscious, to convey the sense of a
space-time-man-god complex, embracing not only the art
of building but all the rest of the life and thought and
belief of their day, is cause for wonder. From this unity
sprang, without doubt, the significance of building forms
we still admire but cannot imitate.

That such a unity of art and life no longer exists needs
no proof. How are we to recapture it? Not surely by imi-
tating or adapting forms evolved from a space-time-man-
god complex that is no longer ours. Not even by means
of new products or structural systems, though we have
passed from the empirical struggle to master space and
span, which once dominated the development of styles,
to the comparative freedom and scientific security of
stress, strain, and the strength of materials. Technics are
important, but only as a means to an end.

The end, if we would recapture unity of art and life
in building, must be to create significant space, whether
real, that is useful and practically dimensioned, or ideal,
that is symbolic and proportionally dimensioned, in
terms of contemporary thought and feeling, not only
socially, economically, and politically, but scientifically,
philosophically, and spiritually. This is the great aim
which the so-called modern school of design, for all its

blind gropings, has set itself. This is functionalism in its broadest interpretation. The building itself becomes a function, in the modern mathematical sense, that is to say, a dependent variable.

It would be presumptuous for an editor to do much commenting or even introducing as preface to the papers in this section. Some readers may feel that too much emphasis has been given to the space-time concept, but surely George Howe makes here the most understandable and appealing statement possible on the difference between the modern understanding of space related to movement and the classic concept of static three-dimensional space. The intellectual and historical exploration of this subject has not been lacking. When Sigfried Giedion followed Alexander's "Space, Time and Deity" and Eddington's "Space, Time, and Gravitation" with his own scholarly "Space, Time and Architecture," there was available the theoretical basis on which to base a space-use technique peculiar to our time. After his paper, Dr. Gropius appends a bibliography which gives some idea of the literature on design principles which is also available.

On the more tangible side, many architects have produced work which illustrates a feeling, conscious or unconscious, for design which permits or even encourages space to flow and move. Yet, despite the hypothesis and the concrete examples, we have yet to discover what Gropius calls a "common denominator" or a "spatial key system" which will be recognizable and socially useful, in the terms that Ames prescribes earlier in the book.

An editor becomes enthusiastic about the material he is working with, and it is possible to exaggerate its importance. Yet it seems fair to say that Howe's description of the "aggregates of planes of reference" and Gropius' translation into the technique of "varying the direction and the tension of component parts of a space composition" begin to approach a new vocabulary of design, which may finally be brought down from the level of intellectual discussion and away from individual attempts at experiment in new forms to a usable and understandable method of composition. Add Wurster's statement on the changing social and technical needs and means, and you have at least an inspiring conception of what buildings could be in this age.

THE BUILDING
IN RELATION TO LARGER SPACE

BY ROBERT B. O'CONNOR

Mr. O'Connor, distinguished architect, Fellow of the American Institute of Architects, sets the theme for the discussion that follows by pointing to the relation of the individual bit of enclosed or limited space—the building—to the topics which have preceded, as well as to the larger concept of the spatial continuum. Mr. O'Connor modestly states the question and then steps aside in deference to the three stimulating papers that follow.

THE Conference so far seems to have brought virtual agreement on several points which we may summarize briefly as follows. To architects the conflict between a traditional and a contemporary approach has all but disappeared in the demands of serious and obviously functional developments. Second, man in the social sense is the urgent problem of man—and of architecture. Third, the machine must be the servant and not the master of man. And finally, the spiritual aspects of man's environment have an even more pervading influence upon him than the physical.

The part which this particular section of the discussion is intended to play is to consider the building as the limiting element in space. Inherent in the modern philosophy of architecture is the belief that a basic aim of design is to relate this individual portion of space which we call the building to its time and place, known in more abstract terms as the spatial continuum. The building, which is usually thought of as the principal concern of architects, has thus been allotted but a small part in these discussions on "Planning Man's Physical Environment." This apparent underemphasis deliberately accentuates the horizons beyond mere enclosing walls which the modern architect must envisage if we are to contribute effectively as a profession to the creation of a happier and more satisfactory human environment.

In the papers which follow, George Howe first outlines the relationship between current trends of mathematical thought and the philosophy of modern architecture. Walter Gropius then expresses the need for a vocabulary of design based upon this philosophy and draws from a scientific knowledge of man's biological and psychological reactions to form what he calls a "counterpoint of space." Finally, William Wurster speaks of the building as a means to an end, namely, modern living with its characteristics of movement and change, rather than as an end in itself.

FLOWING SPACE:
THE CONCEPT OF OUR TIME

BY GEORGE HOWE

George Howe, now engaged on the fourth phase of a remarkable career, is one of the most trenchant commentators on the current architectural scene. Born in Worcester, Massachusetts, in 1886, educated at Harvard and at the École des Beaux Arts, he first practiced as a partner in the firm of Mellor, Meigs & Howe, Philadelphia architects renowned for well-designed traditional work. In 1929 Howe became a partner of William Lescaze, and that firm accomplished work in a very different vein, the outstanding example of which is the office building for the Philadelphia Savings Fund Society. After a period of independent practice he was appointed Supervising Architect for the Public Buildings Administration of the Federal government, a post where he served from 1942 to 1945.

Mr. Howe again is practicing independently, but at the same time serving the cause of good architecture in various consultative capacities. The competition for the design of a memorial site on the St. Louis waterfront to commemorate the

Louisiana Purchase and the nation's expansion westward, sponsored by the Jefferson National Expansion Memorial Association, concluded in February of 1948, was under Howe's able guidance as Architectural Adviser. The program and method of conducting that competition has been applauded generally, and is commented on by Richard Neutra elsewhere in this book. On the conclusion of that assignment, Howe went to Rome as Resident Architect, American Academy in Rome.

In the paper that follows, George Howe does much to bring down to a very understandable level the newer concepts of time and space that have resulted in so many scientific, mathematical, and philosophical discoveries, but which have been slow to affect architecture in any broad sense. As he says, this is "ideal" building space that he discusses; the translation into more specific terms becomes apparent in the papers that follow his.

HAVING meditated on the meaning of space in building design for the last five and a half years, during which I have had plenty of leisure, I now feel like the man described in one of Kafka's diaries, "an expert, a specialist, one who knows his role, a knowledge, to be sure, that cannot be communicated, but which fortunately everyone can do without." Yet, however small the hope of success may be, I persevere in trying to communicate my ideas to others, for, as William the Silent once broke his silence to say, "It is not necessary to hope in order to undertake, nor to succeed in order to persevere."

I must begin by describing the point of view from which I propose to consider the significance of building-space. Building-space can be considered in two ways: first, as the commercial container of human beings, living, laboring, playing, praying; second, as a part, or reduced image, of the universe as men imagine it to be at a given moment in history. In the first sense, building-space may be called real, in the second, ideal. I propose to consider it in its second aspect. Ideal building-space, as the microcosmic embodiment of the cosmos, is the invisible, the mysterious, the numerical, the emanation of the god or gods of its day, the unsubstantial image of the collective unconscious, which, affected from without as well as from within, sets the general pattern of thought and behavior for men of a common heritage.

It is historically observable that the buildings which enjoy the most lasting renown are precisely those which correspond most significantly, in their expression, to the ideal space they limit, both outwardly and inwardly. Take the Greek temple for instance.

The Greek was generally an outward-looking fellow and we find that his temple was designed and built from the outside in, primarily for external effect. Much more technical and esthetic feeling was expended on its peristyle than on the interior scaffolding of stone which supported its slab roof. Its author took little interest in the virtuosities of span and vault which had previously stirred men of other lands, and was to stir them again, to competitive technical emulation.

The temple, like the Grecian Urn, has been admired for its quiet serenity, as a "foster-child of silence and slow time," and we find that the Greek preferred to think of space, and all life with it, as timeless, directionless, restricted. He had no clock until Aristotle invented a clepsydra, after the fall of Athens, and no calendar worthy of the name. He had so little sense of historic continuity that he once signed a treaty to last a hundred years without dating it. His covenants with the gods of heaven and hell were equally devoid of continuity and spatial universality.

The temple has also been admired for its solid geometrical simplicity of form, and we find that the Greek, as modern mathematicians have pointed out, hated the idea of flow and infinity in space. Although Heraclitus, when the temple was still young, had stated that "all is flux," the Greek's mathematical image of space finally stabilized itself in the timeless, directionless, solid geometry of Euclid.

How different is the image of space in our own era, beginning with the Middle Ages. Instead of timeless space we find space-time dominating thought and action from the first. The chiming clock was invented in the century in which the First Crusade was launched, and soon bells were tolling the march of time from towers standing over every hamlet, village, and town. A universal calendar began to be imposed on the world and all events, past, present, future, began to be ordered from the birthday of the only Son of an only God, with whom man was conceived to have entered into an everlasting covenant beginning on that fixed date.

As Romanesque flowered into Gothic, the cathedral choir, suspended, net-like, seems to have been thrown into the air to catch a few of those coordinate points suspended in infinity by which we now represent space to ourselves. It seems to have anticipated analytical geometry and the calculus. On the vault that closed in and defined a small portion of infinite space, the inward-looking western European lavished his technical and esthetic skill, reducing the external elements of stability to a mere scaffolding of stone. As compared to the timeless and directionless temple the cathedral seems almost a temporary structure, corresponding to the concept of perpetual motion and change in space and time.

As the centuries have passed, since the invention of the chiming clock, space-time mathematics, in their practical application to daily life, have destroyed nearly all the dimensions of timeless space. Every problem today becomes a problem of plus and minus acceleration. Motored vehicles have altered the dimensions of town and country; aeroplanes, of the globe. The atom has yielded the secret power of an infinity of infinitesimal tensions to the space-time idea, and the very life of social man has come to be projected graphically along curves of probability.

Penetrated from every side by the radioactivity of our own space-time thought, our physical surroundings are disintegrating before our eyes. Flattened by the bulldozer of our inexorable logic in action, our cities seem to be on the way to becoming desert parking spaces. They must sooner or later be rebuilt to correspond to the image of the universe we have created. For this purpose, we must someday have kinetic money, but that is another question.

All is now flux in very fact: flow of traffic, flow of production, flow of people. Two-faced Janus, god of the threshold and monumental steps, has been banished from industrial and commercial buildings and is about to be banished from government. The iron-studded door of solid oak has given way to invisible Herculite, corresponding to our ideal space, invisible, mysterious, which turns out to be one with real space after all.

Since we find real space is now almost as flowing in fact as ideal space in imagination, we must of necessity give up old timeless ways of thinking about space. Flowing space can be neither enclosed, nor excluded—not even limited, in thought or fact. It can only be directed. It is easy to understand, therefore, that the buildings we call functional, in the sense that they are variables dependent on the values of current thought and action, turn out to be, not objects to be looked at in the light, but aggregates of planes of reference defining the movements, whether in or out or through, of certain portions of universal curvilinear space selected for use as building space. To one who has looked at modern buildings in this way, all the traditional concepts of scale, proportion, façade, grouping, and so forth, become meaningless.

But can aggregates of planes of reference ever be buildings of enduring renown? Only time can tell. Geniuses are now, and have been for fifty years, at work trying to make them so, with some measure of success. In justification of their effort it must be said, at least, that there has never yet been a building of enduring renown that did not correspond more or less closely to the space idea of its day. The Baroque church, palace, and city plan, through insistence on the space idea inherent in the mathematics of Newton and Leibnitz, enjoy a lasting reputation in spite, rather than because, of their denial of structural logic and design discipline. The answer of the functional designer to the question at the beginning of this paragraph must be, therefore: if aggregates of planes of reference cannot be buildings of artistic stature, comparable to that of the past, then there can be no buildings of stature until men return to an older, or evolve a newer, image of the universe.

The traditional designer will stoutly deny this, and his right of denial must be defended to the death, but so must the functional designer's right to his opinion that traditional methods, such as we find around us here, for instance, at Princeton University, are worse than negative in their failure to produce significant form. Collegiate Gothic buildings, Collegiate Georgian buildings, are in fact neither Georgian, nor Gothic, nor even Collegiate in any significant sense, but charnel houses of dead dreams from which the corruption of death filters into the collective unconscious.

A similar opinion was once expressed by George Lansing Raymond, Professor of Esthetic Criticism at Princeton from 1881-1905. After commenting unfavorably on the new Collegiate Gothic buildings at the University, he concluded, "This is said not merely because they are frauds, but because they are—what in art is worse—palpable frauds—donkey's ears protruding where they are clearly seen to have no connection with the body under them."

IN SEARCH
OF A COMMON DENOMINATOR

BY WALTER GROPIUS

Introduced by his first statement on page 41, Walter Gropius adds here a paper on a subject which has long concerned him and other leaders in design progress. He proceeds from the discussion of time and space, goes on to add an important point about the scale which is appropriate to the use of space today, and then comes to the all-important matter of the actual design vocabulary which must result from these theoretical concepts. Dr. Gropius is not a theoretician—he is a designer who has much accomplished work to his credit. Although there have been many attempts to limit his architecture as belonging to a certain "school"—called International Style, or whatever—he himself has always fought free of these moves toward classification and insisted that what he is doing is the development of a *key*—a vocabulary, a common denominator—which is as capable of infinite variations, regional, personal, social, as any other was in other times, with other understandings of the principle of space use. As his students scatter about the world and their work begins to appear, one believes that he has succeeded in that effort.

IT HAS often been said that man's physical surroundings mirror the social, technical, and economic conditions of his period. Changes in the character of the physical surroundings are caused by scientific or technical progress as well as by changes of man's philosophy of life. I am here concerned with man's philosophical outlook which, derived from his spiritual and emotional needs, gives him direction.

The principles of democracy, which put the emphasis on the individual, demand that the design of his physical environment must be in keeping with the human scale. What does that mean?

When the Aztecs or the Egyptians built a pyramid their intention was to create awe and fear of God. An expression of the supernatural through super scale was striven for by the designer. The Caesars, playing god, intending to subjugate their subjects by fear, expressed their power by megalomaniac axes of superhuman scale. Hitler and Mussolini both received in rooms of colossal size, seated at the end opposite the entrance; the approaching visitor was made to feel uneasy and humble.

In a democratic civilization the architect should seek expression of the civic and cultural pride of his community with means other than intimidation. A mature citizen today should react with bored indifference to mammoth-sized structures and space compositions. Yet a space composition—large or small—which is well related to his natural understanding of space and scale will invite and attract him.

If the emphasis today is on the plain human being, not on the Caesars, we have to study man's basic biology, his way of seeing, his perception of distance, in order to grasp what scale will fit him. Buildings should serve his physical and emotional needs, not dictate to him. Their design should avoid all arbitrary physical and psychological barriers. Buildings ought to be means to an end, not ends in themselves; then their scale will be human. This does not limit the greatness of conception nor the dignity of expression; it seeks merely to define the mental tools of the designer. When we perceive space, the size of our body—of which we are permanently conscious—serves as our yardstick or module; that is, our search for the human scale is a search for a finite framework of relationships within the infinite space.

But the relationships in space are not static. They are in constant flux. Our period has discovered the relativity of all human values. Accordingly, the element of time has been introduced as a new dimension in space, and it is penetrating human thought and creation. For instance, in a picture by Picasso we will find both the profile and front of a face depicted. A sequence of views is shown simultaneously. Such an illusion of motion in space in works of architecture, sculpture, and painting is a powerful stimulant. The motion of sunlight and shadows caused by protruding or receding parts of a building gives architecture its life but the intensity of the life of a building is still greatly enhanced when, in addition, the designer creates the illusion of floating space—indoors and outdoors—by varying the direction and the tension of the component parts of his space composition. The acuteness of our senses —which is dulled and lulled by static conditions, perfect as they may be—can be kept awake by skillful design which offers a sequence of arresting surprises in space, which is rich in contrast of tension and repose and well-timed and scaled to satisfy our urge to use our natural functions of adaptation.

With these psychological considerations of the building

as the limiting element of space, we enter the realm of the
architectural creator, who, as a master of the "science of
space," as we may call it, influences the psyche of man. But
can we teach a science of space and design, can we establish
a spatial key system to be used by all as an objective common denominator of design? In music we all are accustomed to a system or an order of the tones to be used as a
conventional key and understood by all; e.g., Bach's well-
tempered clavichord. Of course a key is in no sense a ready-
made formula for a work of art. The shortcut of the brilliant mind is ever needed to create profound art, but a key
provides the impersonal basis as a prerequisite for collective
understanding.

As in music, optical keys were used in past periods of
architecture. The module of the Greeks, the triangulation
of the Gothic builders, served as common denominators to
achieve unity of the physical environment.

Today after a long chaotic period of "l'art pour l'art"—
so utterly unrelated to the collective life of man—a new
language of vision slowly replaces inarticulate individualistic terms like "taste" or "feeling" by terms of greater
objective validity. Based on biological facts—both physical
and psychological—it seeks to represent the impersonal
cumulative experience of successive generations. It offers
first of all the knowledge of optical phenomena as these
are experienced by man. Some examples:

Through irradiation, statues or building parts standing
out against a bright sky appear smaller than they really
are because the bright overspills into the dark. Their size
and volume have to be exaggerated to make them appear
in their intended dimensions.

A baby in the cradle, seeing the moon for the first time
in his life, tries to catch it, for he perceives the reflected
image of the moon only but does not yet know its distance, which has to be learned by individual experience.
When a ceiling is painted in a flat black its height appears
to be less than the actual measurement shows. A wall

painted in a bright yellow seems to move towards us but it recedes when it is painted in a deep blue.

Knowledge of the innumerable optical phenomena in space equips the architect to understand the interrelationship of voids and solids in space, of their direction, their tension or repose, and the psychological value of colors and textures. A solid foundation is thus laid on which many designers can rear a higher embodiment of creative unity.

The true architect stands closer to the philosopher and to the poet than to the scientist, but science provides the architect with the necessary implements to realize his design on an objective basis. The science of space helps him to raise a building beyond its technical and economic conception into the realm of art; it fits him for his prophetic function and enables him to create poetry from words and grammar, that is, from materials and construction. It provides the key for a common language of design to be understood by all.

A science of design and its terminology today are in the stage of development. The Bauhaus started to build up a common denominator of design in its educational methods. Le Corbusier and Ozenfant in *L'Esprit Nouveau*, Moholy-Nagy in *The New Vision* and *Vision in Motion*, Kepes in *Language of Vision*, and others, have contributed to its initial conception.* The further development of this de-

* Dr. Gropius suggests the following bibliography for further study of the subject: *Bauhaus, 1919-1928*, edited by Herbert Bayer, Walter Gropius, Ise Gropius, Museum of Modern Art, New York, 1938; *The New Vision*, by L. Moholy-Nagy, 1928, 3rd revised edition, 1946; *Abstract of an Artist*, by L. Moholy-Nagy, Wittenborn & Co., New York; *Vision in Motion*, Theobald, Chicago, 1947; *L'Esprit Nouveau*, a periodical, Vols. Nos. 1-28, 1920-1925, Paris; *Language of Vision*, by Georgy Kepes with introductory essays by Sigfried Giedion and S. I. Hayakawa, Theobald, Chicago, 1944; *Pedagogical Sketch Book*, by Paul Klee, Nierendorf Gallery, New York, 1944; *L'Art decoratif d'aujourdhui*, by Le Corbusier, Les Éditions G. Cres et Cie., Paris, 1926; *Foundations of Modern Art*, by A. Ozenfant, John Hodker, London, 1931 (a translation of original French edition published by J. Baudry, Paris, 1928); *Punkt und Linie zue Flache*, by W. Kandinsky, Bauhausbucher Vol. 9, Albert Langen, Munich; *Précisions*, by Le Corbusier, Les Éditions Cres, Paris; *Almanach d'architecture moderne*, by Le Corbusier, Les Éditions Cres, Paris.—Ed.

sign key appears to be highly desirable for better architectural education. It will lead us out of the confusion of sentimental remembrances towards constructive creative architecture.

THE NEED FOR CHANGE

BY WILLIAM W. WURSTER

Dean of the School of Architecture and Planning at the Massachusetts Institute of Technology, William Wurster is both an outstanding architect and an educator who has strongly influenced recent trends in the architectural schools. He was born in California in 1895, educated at the University of California (and much later as a Fellow in Harvard's Graduate School of Design), practiced architecture alone and in association with others, and assumed his present position of Dean in 1945. He still maintains a professional interest in both seacoasts and a hand in actual practice as partner in the San Francisco firm of Wurster, Bernardi & Emmons. Wurster is commonly pointed to by architectural critics as an architect who has carried the California tradition of a regional contemporary expression, stated first perhaps by Maybeck, on into the present period. There is no doubt that his influence on the younger generation of architects who are concerned with what he calls in the following paper "the spiritual and creative aspect" of design has been important and beneficial.

In his comments below Dean Wurster, admittedly more "pedestrian" than either Howe or Gropius, investigates briefly the factors calling for movement and change in the design of buildings for our time—social and technical factors consistent with the modern time and space concepts that have been described in the preceding statements.

THE preceding papers have dealt with the subject of "the building as the limiting element of space" in the broadest sense, both historically and in the very essence of building. George Howe has even captured timelessness, which will make any further statement seem pedestrian. Yet I would like to list a very few specific things that emerged in my thinking as I considered the question: "What has brought the greatest change in the character of buildings in our time?"

The characteristic influence which distinguishes buildings of this age, it seems to me, is *movement* and the very *need* for change. At the same time we do not want to accomplish this change at the sacrifice of any human safety factor such as fireproofing, nor do we want to increase the difficulty of upkeep.

This movement, or need for change, results from many factors. First we might list *social changes*: less permanent family relationships; fewer children in the family unit; more rapidly changing jobs, both in location and type of employment; even the desire of a family for movement within the metropolitan area to give children more space at certain ages.

Next we might list *transportation changes*—the effect of the automobile and the airplane. Actual planning has not even begun to consider the influence of the airplane on our building forms, and the results of automobile transportation are causing confusion. For example, because of it the entire shopping pattern changes. There is more drastic change on its way when building owners are compelled to care for storage of automobiles on their own property, so that the streets may again become thoroughfares and no longer be used as parking lots. This may lift our whole building program up an entire floor; perhaps the way to achieve it will be calmly to take all our present streets and regard them as subways, with the new streets one story higher. Motor transport has, in fact, already had an effect on buildings. New hotels have their entrances buried in the center of the building, where cars can more comfortably drop their passengers. The Pentagon building outside Washington was planned for busses and automobiles to drive into and under the building. There, as in other instances, the porticoed entrance is merely a vestigial architectural remnant.*

* There was some further discussion of this subject at the Conference. Morris Ketchum spoke of the importance, which we are likely to forget, that

A third factor inducing change in building forms is the important one of *mechanical change*. Every item of advance here spells fewer hours spent in human drudgery. For example, electricity lights our homes with no cleaning of lamps; gas does our cooking with its flexible, flowing delivery; oil heats our houses with no labor expended. We can foresee further than this; even snow shoveling may pass if we use panel heat to clear our sidewalks, as Carl Koch has done on the Snake Hill Road.

Closely related to the mechanical changes are improvements in the *materials* of building, permitting a limitless variety of forms, with our desires no longer so quickly curbed. Think of the great glass areas possible. We no longer need hibernate in winter, with the fear of cold and costly heating. Think of the open living which is now permitted—we can partake visually in the beauty of each day, see the clouds and the trees against the sky.

---

pedestrian traffic still has in the design of shopping centers. Talbot Hamlin added the following comment on the same subject: "The importance of *pedestrian* traffic, both practically and esthetically, is currently underrated. Perhaps the aim of much city planning should be not to make more and faster automobile traffic possible but to make it neither necessary nor desirable by arranging the largest amount of safe and pleasant pedestrian circulation. If a careful time analysis were made of the total amount of time spent outdoors either walking or riding in cars by all the individuals in a community—an investigation, which, I believe, has never been made —I am sure it would show a vast preponderance of walking time. Even in families who own a car, if the time of *all* the members of the family were taken, I am sure the same result would be true. Would it not, then, be the part of true democratic planning to make the pedestrian circulation the chief element instead of, as it usually is, a mere secondary consideration? Certainly the pouring of hundreds of millions of dollars into parkways and freeways has produced a condition under which the advantages of a minority of the people are paid for by the taxes of a majority of the people, especially in large cities.

"The esthetic recognition of the pedestrian scale is also of the greatest importance. When one is hurrying by in a automobile, buildings are a blur. When one is strolling by them, they become either a blessing or a curse, individually or as a group, for one really sees them. The most important esthetic consideration in the exterior design of a housing group, it seems to me, is the effect it makes upon the children who play in it, the housewife walking to the corner grocery, or the people who sit in its resting spaces on a summer evening."—Ed.

But the most important thing of all, the thing that has emerged again and again at this Conference, is the human spirit—the spiritual and creative aspect of the design of buildings. Considering this factor in relation to changes in building forms, I say—let us have less permanence; let us give each generation the creative joy which has been ours, and let us not expect them to enjoy our outworn shells. Marble and permanence—what a burden they have placed upon the world! Think of the intricacy of most of the buildings created by recent generations. How can we expect fresh, clear thoughts to emerge from the very educational centers, now in use, which were designed thus?

Let us join with those who gave the following epitaph to Van Brugh of Blenheim fame: "Lie heavy upon him, O earth, for he has laid many a heavy thing upon thee."

SECTION VII

INSPIRATION
AND PRAGMATISM

INTRODUCTION

BY THOMAS H. CREIGHTON

T HE papers in this section of the book may seem out of character with the others that have preceded them. However, this is a symposium, and many points of view are represented. Frank Lloyd Wright and Robert Moses have contributed interesting statements of position—in places brilliant, in each case containing some opinions which are certain to be antagonistic to any point of view the reader may hold.

The final session of the Princeton Conference was a dinner, at which the principal speakers were Wright and Moses. It was the thought of those who had arranged the proceedings that these two would attend the other sessions as well, and that their remarks on the final night would be a summation in terms of the two opposed (or parallel) planes of accomplishment on which the planning of man's physical environment must be carried out—the individual inspired genius (seeing from above the belt with a natural mind, as Wright defines it) and the slow, plodding, sometimes bureaucratic method of political pragmatism.* However, neither man attended any of the sessions at which other people read papers, and hence their remarks have little relation to the themes which had been developing during the Conference. And they represent two such sharp extremes that each seems to be stating his own position, not a typical one, with the great area of democratic accomplishment in planning and building by men who are neither geniuses nor bureaucrats falling somewhere between or outside the two.

Perhaps, for some readers who are not completely famil-

* Mr. Wright wrote to Arthur Holden, accepting the invitation to speak, that he was "glad to be some of the 'real meat' of the Conference. But what part of the carcass I am not so sure. Moses and I are somewhat in the category of Jack Benny and Fred Allen, or Shaw and Wells, I guess. So I may be off the hind quarter. We'll see."

iar with the tremendous accomplishments and voluminous writings of these two articulate generators, the preceding paragraph needs amplification. Frank Lloyd Wright, who is now as used to being called today's greatest architect as he is to being ignored in planning councils, cannot be considered in any way "typical" of the individual brilliant practitioner. Genius is never typical. And Wright could never be typical of anything, because as soon as one or two people seem to be on the point of catching up with him, he pulls himself away from them either by the quality of his creative design or by some arbitrary, often insulting, expression of personal individuality. (At Princeton he said, "I have been accused of having contempt for my fellow architects—I have no contempt for them; only for their work.") His concern for democracy is great and real, but it is translated immediately into his own planning conception —Broadacre City. The conception is an organic and an exciting idea, which has so stimulated many young people who have had the opportunity to study under Wright that they have gone forth as missionaries. But the point here is that it is a personal one—you either accept it whole, or you have no place alongside the master. I am sure that there will be many people who could applaud nine-tenths of Wright's paper that follows, but will gag violently on the remaining tithe. Perhaps it will be the comment that he believes "were all education above the high school level suspended for ten years humanity would get a better chance to be what humanitarian Princeton itself could wish it to be." Perhaps it will be his recommendation that we do not send more G.I.'s, by way of government money that they will repay themselves or their children will repay, to school. No, as an outstanding individual, in architecture and in philosophy, Wright cannot be considered to state any position but his own. That makes his own statement all the more readable.

Robert Moses occupies an individual spot for other reasons. Holding government positions which have given him authority to accomplish widespread urban redevelopment, he condemns wide-outlook planning. Believing strongly in the concept of individual initiative, he has written many articles poking fun at individual planning ideas. He points with pride to the fact that he has "had to fight for everything" he has accomplished, and yet he inclines to sneer at those who fight for ideas. He is a man of action; he has said "it is not knowledge but action which is the great end and objective in life . . . for every dozen men with bright ideas there is at most one who can execute them."* And still he seems to distrust action which will implement ideas: his preference is to "modify, adapt, and improvise." His attitude inevitably leads him to condemnation of contemporary expressions in architecture—his position on this question is well known and has been expressed many times; at Princeton it comes forward in an approval of the college structures there as producing "a conservative and classical atmosphere, on a campus and amidst buildings of fine and enduring, if old and imitative architecture." This is a far cry from the consideration of design on social, technical, philosophical, psychological, and esthetic bases in the preceding portions of the book. And yet it cannot be considered a statement typical of the more conservative architects and planners—it is Moses' own.

And so we have three papers in this section—Frank Lloyd Wright's original talk, the statement by Robert Moses, and finally a transcript of informal remarks that Wright made following Moses, amusing and somewhat penetrating comments on the difference between the individual who soars and the individual who grubs.

* *New York Times Magazine*, March 7, 1948.

EDUCATION, INDIVIDUALISM, AND ARCHITECTURE

BY FRANK LLOYD WRIGHT

No individual has had a stronger or more salutary effect on architecture in our time than Frank Lloyd Wright. Since his first executed commission in 1893 until his most recently published projects he has continued to contribute fresh and sensible ideas in design conception, planning, adaptation to the site, use of materials, structural systems, and social usefulness.

His reference to Louis Sullivan in the paper that follows hints at the relationship between the two; when Wright left the University of Wisconsin, where he had studied engineering, he worked in Adler and Sullivan's office in Chicago for some seven years. His own early work cut through the tasteless design that was then typical of the Midwest, and resulted in houses that still seem to "belong" to their properties. He has gone on from one commission to another—his best known work includes the Imperial Hotel in Tokyo, the office building for the Johnson Wax Company in Racine, Wisconsin, the Kaufmann house near Pittsburgh, Pennsylvania, known as Falling Water, and his own homes (both called Taliesin) and workshops at Spring Green, Wisconsin, and in the desert near Phoenix, Arizona— with so much experimentation that no "style label" other than "organic" could possibly be applied to him. There is a feeling of organic unity throughout his designs and between the structure and the site which is common to them all—he calls this work "organic" architecture.

Wright has written a great deal. His *An Autobiography* (Duell, Sloan and Pearce, N.Y., 1943) has probably been his most influential book; the most recent, *When Democracy Builds* (University of Chicago Press, Chicago, 1945). The Kahn lectures at Princeton, to which he refers below, were published under the title of *Modern Architecture* (Princeton University Press, 1931).

MY FAVORITE university is Princeton. Memory of pleasant times here long ago while delivering the Kahn lectures brings me now from Arizona desert to anticipated Princetonian revels of intellectual fellowship. I have the same nostalgic love for Princeton as for the great founders of our

Republic. And yet, I believe, were all education above the high school level suspended for ten years humanity would get a better chance to be what humanitarian Princeton itself could wish it to be. Our thinking throughout the educational fabric has been so far departmentalized, overstandardized, and so split that like a man facing a brick wall counting bricks, we mistake the counting for reality—and so lose or ignore the perspective that would show us the nature and wherefore of the wall as a wall.

As a people we are—no doubt—educated far beyond our capacity. We have urbanized urbanism until it is a disease —the city a vampire living upon the fresh blood of others, sterilizing the humanity for which you, Princeton, have always stood. And now this cataclysm, the atom bomb of science, has thrown us off our base, undoubtedly making all we have been calling progress obsolete overnight. Prone to our own destruction, we may be crucified upon our own cross! To me, an architect, this further revelation of the nature of the industrial mechanistic universe we inhabit as parasites or gods (it is up to us) has been a ghastly revelation of the failure of our educational, economic, and political systems. The push-button civilization over which we were gloating has suddenly become a terror. But instead of the agony appropriate in the actual circumstances, we are even more smug and heedless than usual. A little flurry—that's all. The military mind is a dead mind—so, no surprise to find its reaction what it was. The journalistic mind, a reporter's mind, left to the humorist the only real attempt to arouse the people to its reality: not an explosive bomb only, but a fantastic poison-bomb that made their habitation in cities no safer than an ant-hill beneath a ploughshare in a field.

So, my Princeton, I say, let's pause and consider this lack of vision that not only hides from us the better nature of ourselves but makes us unable to see any further than our own furrows. Weighed down by our own armor, insatiate with this voracity we call speed, huddled the more—though not suitably—in panic, it is conceivable that the country we now call ours may go back to the Indians. Escaping the ultimate explosion—the probable apex of our civilization —as they will, they might easily come and take it back again, quietly in the night, proving that barbarism is, after all, better suited to human life here on earth than what we have too carelessly called civilization.

In this fearful emergency, the State as such has proved utterly unworthy the allegiance accorded it by the sons and friends of American education. Politics, in any perspective afforded it by this insensate clamor and clash of power-seekers exploiting the Almighty Dollar is sadly in need not only of the brief recess of ten years or more, but the utter abolition of the State Department and the Presidency as both now exist. We should strip the Capitol from the periphery of the nation and plant it nearer the heart of the country itself. In our education, we must realize there can be no real separation of religion, philosophy, science, and the great art of building. They are one or none. But in this petty partisan particularity now everywhere so prevalent we find education itself the more divided into petty specialties, and those most advantageous to the ignoble profit and party system we have so foolishly made the very core of our republican life.

So let us rise for a moment from the furrow to take the view; and soon, with disgust, we will dismiss petty politics for the prostitution it is now become. Instead, let us view excess urbanism . . . this pig-piling or human huddling we call the city. It is true that to very many the city is a stimulus similar to alcohol, ending in similar degeneracy or impotence—no city can maintain itself by way of its own birth rate for more than three years—and a glance at history will show us that all civilizations have died of their cities. To others like our good old Doctor Johnson, the city is a convenience because every man is so close to his burrow. But read "hole in the wall" now for "burrow." Nevertheless, the American city of the industrial revolution was out of date for our humanity long before the cataclysmic poison-bomb of the chemical revolution appeared on the horizon to clinch the argument.

Then, how now? Are not further concentrations of humanity madness or murder? We must remember the Hindu proverb, "A thousand years a city and a thousand years a forest." UN is, of course, the present hope for escape and survival. But UN itself has taken refuge in a New York skyscraper! Can it make good with that symbol?

And we must review education, wherein the salt and savor of "work as gospel" is gone out. The elaborate gymnasium has taken its place. The higher education itself is busy taking everything apart, strewing the pieces about in an effort to find what makes it all tick; failing to put it together again it cannot make it click. It cannot because it cannot or will not go back with an *organic* point of view to begin on anything at all. So education itself, like the city planning by long-haired experts for short-haired moles, is either a noisy splash in the middle of something—or else a short strand of some particular color in a tangled skein of colored worsted. Continuity and unity? They are gone. So inorganic education is almost as helpless to confront this ghastly emergency we are blindly refusing to face as is the inorganic state.

Next, if not in order, let us view our ethics. Men born free and equal? Before the law they should be so—yes, perhaps—but the coming man does not believe that all men are born free and equal in point of quality because he cannot. As a millennial aspiration? Yes, to accept it as a truth would only be dangerous because a world so planned implies total death. Consistent struggle makes our world what it is—not struggle for equality but for spiritual supremacy. That struggle is in the very process of creation, inequality is the basis of the creative process. In the brain lies the chief difference between men. Only a state politician out for reelection at a Fourth of July picnic could say we are all born with the same brain-power and yet freedom is the true and only safeguard for mankind whatever his degree. His valid protection.

Let us now glance askance at our busy "production." Naturally, everybody, everywhere, cannot be taught to love, appreciate, and assimilate art or religion or to comprehend the nature of anything. It is impossible to impart to any man one single grain of truth unless he has the undeveloped germs of it within himself. Buddha said, "A spoon may lie in the soup for a thousand years and never know the flavor of the soup." So far as education is concerned, only when the heart is open is it fit to receive teaching quick with life. Eyes must be there as well as ears, and be opened first before illusion, superstition, or prejudice may be expelled. Architecture, the great Mother Art, is in itself the highest knowledge-in-action of which we have any record and cannot be bought or ever acquired from books. One good look at an actual building, and a man has found what no reams of writing or years of teaching could give him—providing he has the eyes to see.

And what are our buildings? Education and two wars have all but killed the germ of creative thinking. And so creative work for us—especially in building—is all but destroyed. This amazing avalanche of material we call production seems to have its eyes shut to all but destruction. The standardizations we practice now are the death of the soul, just as habituation kills any imaginative spirit. So within this welter of the misapplied wealth of knowledge, wherein consideration, kindness, and truth are so rare, why not develop a little integral *know-how*? Only spirit affords that.

Now come our G.I.'s, themselves survivors all but destroyed by the army, to be further devastated by four more years of education. Why send more G.I.'s, by way of government money they will themselves repay (or their children will repay) to school? Why not subsidize land and transportation for them to relieve intolerable immediate pressures instead of sending them back to hard pavements, to trample or be trampled upon further by the civilian herd? Why not get the boys out where they can get in touch with and be touched by their own birthright: the good ground? Give each man an open chance at acreage to make his own environment beautiful, if possible. Restore to him what he most needs: the right to be himself! If unable to build, owing to the false doctrines of artificial controls or of economic scarcity—making and maintaining our black markets now—why not throw natural roads open to immigration from countries where the skills have not been cut back by ignorant labor unions emulating their still more ignorant employers with their doctrines of economic scarcity? The only requirements for immigration to our democratic society should now be common decency and trade skills. Then not only would the G.I. learn from them and by the natural working of the law of supply and demand have a home, but all America would soon have better homes and have them according to their own efforts.

No!—no assembly-line is the answer either for him, for you, or for me (and that means for our country) in education, building or living. Decentralization of our American cities and intelligent utilization of our own ground, making natural resources available to him for subsistence, is his road, yours and mine, to any proper future as a democracy for which we may reasonably hope. Essentially, we are a mob-ocracy now. Our present extreme centralization is a bid to slavery—all down the line, a bid-in by a shortsighted, all too plutocratic industrialism in control of government.

But the right to strike still belongs to the American people as well as to American labor unions. The time has come for that strike. I find it increasingly hard to believe that a free people can be so blinded to the nature of their own power as our people have been by their own foolish credulity. Why do they want to keep their eyes shut?

What remedy? No remedy will be found in more statism. That is only more static, truly. More must come from the people themselves. The remedy is more freedom, greater growth of individuality and protection for it—more men developed by way of self-discipline from within by the man himself. Today, especially, the most cowardly lie disseminated by the congenital cowards among us, as well as by the Church, School, and State, is this lie that "I, the State, am the people!" In a democracy where the people remains a people, the people do not understand the State any more than the superstition that the people call "Money." In a true democracy the people are bound to only suffer the State as against their own customs and natural rights. Democracy cannot love government! Government is its policeman, privileged by the people themselves to obstruct, expropriate, or punish. Under the watchful care of the people themselves government must take its place down *under*, not up above the right of the individual to be himself.

No executive should ever be allowed to become a popular hero—or make our policy for us. We need a strong body of high-minded independent citizens first to frame policy—then find the executive not only in name but in fact to put this policy into execution. We will then soon be on the way to a remedy. The Organic State.

PUBLIC AND PRIVATE INITIATIVE

BY ROBERT MOSES

At present Robert Moses is New York City's Park Commissioner. The list of official positions he has held is an impressive one: it includes terms as Chief of Staff of New York State Reconstruction Commission, President of Long Island State Park Commission, Chairman of State Council of Parks, Secretary of State of New York State, Chairman of the Jones Beach State Park Commission, and many others.

In these positions Moses has been largely responsible for the carrying out—and often the conception—of many park and beach development projects, major trafficways including parkways, bridges, and tunnels, and many other reclamation and urban redevelopment jobs. He has been retained as planning consultant by cities other than New York. He likes to be known, as his paper indicates, as a man of action rather than ideas, and yet he has found time to do much writing and lecturing. He was Centennial Lecturer at Duke University in

1939, Godkin Lecturer at Harvard in the same year, and Stafford Little Lecturer at Princeton in 1940. His published articles have covered a wide range of planning and administrative topics; on occasion they have been extremely critical of those he considers theoretical planners (particularly those born outside the United States, for whom he coined the word *beiunskis*) and of current architectural developments.

YOU have asked me to speak in the role of a public official on public and private cooperation to improve man's physical environment. I appear on this occasion as a timid, inhibited representative of the Philistine or lowest common denominator. My distinguished contemporary, Frank Lloyd Wright, on the other hand, enjoys all the privileges and immunities of an individualist responsible only to his conscience and his God. In such a debate—if debate it is— all the advantages are manifestly with the Sage of Taliesin and Paradise Valley.

The proximate aim of debate is the sharp presentation of divergent opinions, not the discovery of common ground, which should follow. It may therefore be assumed that I am neither as hopeless a Philistine nor as uncompromising an enemy of the children of light as this evening's talk may indicate. Frank Lloyd Wright and I approach somewhat the same objectives from very different roads, with perhaps the further reservation that he aims higher and farther. One of our gifted minor Yale poets, in verses still more popular when I was in college, said it all very neatly and modestly:

Brother in hope, if you
Should ever pierce our empyrean through;
And find that radiant star,
Whose Beams we have not seen, yet know they are;
Say that I loved it, too,
But could not climb so far.

The gap which has so long yawned between public and private initiative is in a certain rather obvious, and therefore not profound, sense narrowing, if indeed it is not closing entirely. I should be less than frank if I did not admit some serious misgivings over this geological phenomenon, and some apprehension that the menacing social and economic quakes and tremors which agitate the world today may cause greater cleavages as well as heal breaches in our body politic.

There are vast spaces on our globe where pretty nearly everyone works for the government. There private initiative, in the sense in which we in America use the phrase, has dried up and opposition to the corporate public will is liquidated. It may be that Frank Lloyd Wright can explain convincingly why a system so sterile and intolerant of freedom is at the moment so hospitable to modern talent in the arts and crafts. The phenomenon has puzzled wiser heads than mine.

As for me, give me liberty with all its connotations, pleasant and unpleasant, stimulating and irksome, rather than that death of the spirit which is bound to be visited on those who live under an exclusive and all-powerful government. By the same token, I should rather work in the maddening and infuriating atmosphere of American politics, and accept the rules, risks, and uncertain rewards of the game as we play it, than receive an iron-clad commission from a dictator coupled with the assurance that any nitwit, grafter, or interloper who got in my way would be strung to the nearest lamp post, exiled, or "spurlos versenkt." This is the way I feel tonight and in my better and more reflective moods. There have been, I admit, times when a few broken heads and bloody noses, brought about in the interest of progress, have not seemed entirely unjustified.

This passing reference to mayhem and violence brings me logically to an observation which the academic mind, for some curious reason, hesitates to accept. Life is competitive, and, please God, will continue to be so in these United States for a long time to come. I cannot conceive of politics, government, administration, physical progress, and even the coordination of public and private enterprise in any other terms. I have had to fight for everything I have been able to accomplish and, in spite of extraordinary assistance and loyalty, the results have not been obtained easily, or by diplomacy, sleight of hand, logic, eloquence, and the charm upon which so many philosophers depend.

Nevertheless, I have no thought of disturbing your digestive processes by tales of dated exploits and battles long ago, but I can say this and challenge any man here successfully to deny it, that unless you have a combative instinct, a stomach for a fight, and a willingness to argue your case with the press and the people, you won't go very far in changing our American environment for the better. It will not be done by soft words, and in the process you will have to meet on the most outrageous and unfair terms the smooth writer, the demagogue, the reactionary, the standpatter, the glib promiser, the rabble-rouser, the sloth, the fox, and the lone wolf.

Water does not rise above its own level, and government cannot be much better than the people who make it. As a matter of fact, I sometimes think that the people get better government than they are entitled to, considering the proverbial ingratitude of republics and the speed with which democracy tires of its leading personalities. The young American who goes into the fascinating field of public business must expect little pay, uncertainty, insecurity even in the higher brackets of the civil service, small recognition, frequent misrepresentation, but also the many satisfactions of accomplishment, a part in raising the standards and improving the environment of our children, and finally experimentation in a fascinating laboratory.

Now there are decided limits to experimentation. Not long ago in New York City, my friend Rex Tugwell, as Chairman of the City Planning Commission, offered a master plan of our five boroughs in which vast spaces aggregating about a third of our entire acreage were cross-hatched and designated as "greenbelts." The phrase "greenbelts" is one of those bits of professional planning jargon previously associated with the Resettlement Administration. Our New York City greenbelts were, it seems, to be sown with parks,

gardens, landscaped open spaces and vistas. Existing ex-
crescences and non-conforming uses were to be blotted out
in the way that a tough commanding general issues an order
of the day declaring certain hot spots out of bounds for the
boys. Dr. Tugwell sought, in effect, to declare a third of
the City not only badly planned, but worthless for the purposes for which it was being used. At the same time, har-
assed tax commissioners were busy proving that these
properties were underassessed and much more valuable
than the owners admitted.

What the courts in certiorari proceedings would have
done with such an issue, confronted by two sets of contend-
ing officials approaching land uses and values from utterly
different and irreconcilable viewpoints, is something for the
judicious to ponder. Fortunately, the master greenbelt plan
blew up, and its author moved on to greener fields in the
Caribbean. Here again he had an opportunity to demonstrate the effectiveness of what he called the "Fourth
Power"—that is, government planning—and here again it
was shown that you cannot improve man's environment by
attempting to force on him systems not in keeping with
local tradition and psychology. The native Caribbean dictator is a revolutionist only for purposes of accession.
Thereafter he becomes ultraconservative, goes in for both
solid and showy public works, and tolerates no democratic
nonsense.

There are, to be sure, capitalists who are just as extreme,
and often as intolerant in opposing government regulation
and initiative as are the Fourth Power advocates who would
reduce every businessman to a despised Kulak. I am a prag-
matist in such matters. There is no principle which decides
for us just where the line is fixed between the bureaucrat
and the businessman, or between and among federal, state,
and municipal governments. Pragmatism is to planning
what relativity is to physics. Man is in the grip of new forces
which he has recently discovered, but is as yet unable to
control. What we all need is free trade, not necessarily in
goods, but in brains. The worst barriers are those of stupid

prejudice. The best imports and exports are ideas, even if they are at variance.

Rex Tugwell once called me a "compartment socialist," by which epithet he meant that I was a true liberal only about parks and playgrounds. Well, that was a shrewd observation, because I firmly believe that there are services which government alone can provide, others which require close teamwork by public and private enterprise, and still others which are the function of business. Dr. Tugwell thinks that the Fourth Power, composed of planning pundits appointed for life and superior to the executive, legislative, and judicial functions, should map our entire future. There Rex and I part company for keeps.

Since Hiroshima and Nagasaki, the advocates of urban decentralization have embraced the new major premise of early, inevitable, and inescapable atomic destruction of all concentrated industry and society. Before we abandon our present civilization with its manifest imperfections and return to the caves and huts of our ancestors, I suggest that we exhaust the tenets of faith and religion, the arts of diplomacy, the sanctions of law and economics, the dictates of common sense and the fundamental decency of the average man.

Most of us must accept with enthusiasm, resignation, or regret, as the case may be, the inheritances of the past, and in our planning aim to modify, adapt, and improvise rather than raze, dynamite, and revolutionize. I hate compromise more than most public officials, but I realize that it is at once the curse and the glory of the democratic process. He who wrestles to some purpose with the physical problems of an old and stubborn city or mushroom suburb deserves, in my poor opinion, somewhat more credit than the builder of a Canberra in the wilderness, the architect of a new town ordered by an ambitious benevolent dictator or evoked from the wilderness by a progressive American corporation operating on foreign soil with cheap, native labor. I must admit, however, that no public body or private patron has as yet endowed me with the power and money to do one of those *de novo*, blank-slate jobs which seem to fall so invitingly into the lap of genius.

When Kubla Khan decrees a stately pleasure dome, Frank Lloyd Wright or Le Corbusier is sent for. I get into the picture when there is a remote, disputed barrier beach, an abandoned salt meadow, or a rundown, ragged, misused shore front to be reclaimed, a narrow parkway right-of-way to be torn foot by foot from reluctant, embattled, and avaricious estate owners and subdividers, or a forlorn gashouse and slum to be carved out with an axe or scalpel.

It takes more than two or three decades of untiring effort to achieve anything of neighborhood importance, not to speak of regional consequence, in and around an old, populous, highly-assessed and normally resistant city. The public official who is allowed to remain long enough in office to do it is fortunate indeed. His head may be bloody, but it is unbowed. Without even remotely challenging his achievements, I take pride in having beaten Baron Haussman's service record in Paris. He lasted only seventeen years. With the generous support of mayors and governors and others, I have been able in some instances to make the interference, if nothing else, for the men, many of them anonymous and unrecognized, and all of them inadequately rewarded, who are responsible for most of our New York City and State improvements.

No doubt these small accomplishments are mere piecemeal palliatives, escape corridors, puerile makeshifts, and poultices in the eyes of those to whom every big city is a curse and an anachronism, and every limited improvement merely a futile effort to prolong intolerable conditions. The practical people with whom my lot is cast work with the instruments, the resources, and the powers at hand to accomplish what we can in our time, and leave the prophecies of doom and the purple passages of derision to those who take it out in talk and printer's ink.

A real general who directs strategy, albeit from the comparative safety of G.H.Q., has my profound respect, which does not, however, extend to the philosophical scribbler with no combat record, no commission, no authority, no risk, and no responsibility, who thunders in the index or squeaks and mutters in the press about the folly and futility of piecemeal, tactical warfare. At every shooting gallery or rifle range there is a kibitzing sidewalk superintendent who never touches a gun, but jibes that the targets are too close, the sights not sufficiently high, and that hitting the bull's eye is no more impressive than heaving a brick at a wall.

When all is said and done, the improvement of our environment, like every other human enterprise, depends upon leadership, and leadership is partly a matter of education and partly a God-given quality which has little relation to anything we can analyze or control. It is peculiarly fitting that Princeton at its Bicentennial should be the scene of this discussion, because Princeton has a splendid and unbroken record of training for public service to which that great educator, political scientist, executive and evangelist, Woodrow Wilson, so often and so proudly referred. At Yale we set out with a similar goal, for our charter declared that it was our primary purpose to educate young men "for publick employment both in Church & Civil State." May this tradition be sustained and nourished in these twins of learning for many centuries to come.

How can the lesson be lost on any discriminating person that this tradition has flourished here in Princeton, in a conservative and classical atmosphere, on a campus and amidst buildings of fine and enduring, if old and imitative architecture? Are not aspiration and tradition the greatest of all functions of the church and the university, and should not these noble objectives be reflected in plan and architecture? Is not this, the highest type of functionalism, even more important than the convenience of the clergy and faculty, and the comfort of parishioners and students? Is the iconoclast quite unabashed in the home of the eternal verities? How can we ignore here the conclusion that we should hold on to what has served us well and nobly in the past until we find something surely and probably better? Beauty is timeless, but change is the rule of existence. There is really no inherent conflict between tradition and innovation. The sound and solid, as distinguished from the freakish, egotistical innovation of today is the tradition of tomorrow.

This brings me back full circle to the beginning. We must continue to dwell and work in a competitive and changing world. Those of us who lean a little to the right ask only that the revolutionaries prove the worth and durability of their ideas and products before they demand universal acceptance. What could be fairer than that? And if the monotonous horizontal planes, the severe, functional façades, the lally columns, spirals, discs, and cantileverings of modern architecture shall perchance survive for centuries and shall delight the eye of graduate and undergraduate, town and gown, as have the traditional Gothic and Georgian structures which are here celebrating their bicentennial, may I express the pious hope that the surfaces of these brash inventions be mantled and overgrown with the toughest, greenest, most soothing, and most charitable ivy?

THE MOLE AND THE SKYLARK

BY FRANK LLOYD WRIGHT

On the conclusion of the prepared papers by Wright and Moses, the subject was thrown open for "discussion" from the floor. Very little was forthcoming. William Wilson Wurster protested that neither of the two statements was in the spirit of the Conference, and hoped that they would in no way be taken as summation (newspaper publicity did, inevitably, concentrate on the more controversial remarks made by various speakers) and George Howe made a few amusing remarks. Other than that there was no reaction from the distinguished group present. Not wishing to let the occasion die so quickly, Wright spoke informally in the words that follow.

FOR at least fifty-three years of actual practice I have worked away at this affair of planning man's physical en-

vironment, meantime believing that only as the integrity
of a noble spirit was reflected by it—even projected in it—
could a free people have a civilization worthy the Democratic ideal of Freedom.

A witty Frenchman whose name I should remember—I
have quoted him so often—said ours is "the only great nation to have proceeded directly from barbarism to degeneracy with no civilization of our own in between." Lifelong
I have been trying to do something about that missing civilization—something that would invalidate the witty
Frenchman's thrust.

A friendly little note reached me while in Arizona from
Moses the Mole (from somewhere in South America, I
think) and referring to our coming meeting on this occasion he said, "We were all after the same thing really, each
in his own way." That's true, and I guess nearly everybody
is in his own way. But what a difference in the way! Now
as for getting after this proof of culture which we call environment, it is the different way in which we get it that is
important. But more important still is to *work* for it. And
few are content to *work* as hard for it as the "Robert-
Moses." I am in no position here to brag of my share in the
great work. I have observed that most of the infestors of
our environment are quite content to steal their share in it
or climb on the other fellow's shoulders to take a ride
whichever way the affair seems at the time to be going;
others read up on the affair and as bystanders look on—
pleased or disgusted critics. Still others, having been to Oxford or American derivatives, nominate the appropriate
styles their Education (so-called) may have approved. A
sorry if not truly sordid state of affairs. Now Bob (the
Mole) and I are friendly enemies, perhaps we would better
say inimical friends: you all know the man who didn't have
an enemy in the world but whose friends didn't like him.
Not that Bob has not a flourishing crop of enemies, but I
prefer mine to his. He brags that he is a Mole and says I am
a Skylark. Meaning, of course, that he is down there doing
all the work while I mount and sing myself away. I want to

call his attention here to the fact that we have been unable to domesticate this European bird in America so I refer you all to Wordsworth's "To a Skylark"; a ground-loving, ground-nesting bird. Rising straight up into the sky inspired by what he feels within him and sees, he sings his heart straight out. You see the Lark is not content down there nesting just above the Mole (he may eat one now and then for all I know) because the Lark has what we call— Vision! At this point, I might refer you to Schopenhauer on the Mole. But why? The fact remains that, Skylark or Mole, however much environment we try to cover or create with indefatigable energy, science, or horsepower, it can never add up to the spiritual circumstance of a true environment for a democratic civilization unless we square ourselves with this affair above the belt which we call the *Individual*, free and therefore truly creative. No! Because it is one troublesome characteristic of power in the hands of forceful men that when their first-rate great force is expended they are prone to the influence of seconds and culls. That is to say either to the prejudiced or pretenders. What their power ultimately does turn up is too apt to be either the falsity of the downright ugly or the mincing of the unduly refined. To me this—their trait— (it may be no more) is utterly a shameful waste of raw material. Seeing it undiminished in the Mole is a weariness of the Skylark soul. Moles should forego opinions on songs even though they had ears to hear. They do not have eyes with which to see. And, no less, all Larks when they leave the ground to sing should keep their attention on where they are going, not just be content to see where they have been. Both Mole and Lark, I'm sure, are component parts of any sane move toward a nobler environment for man. Both should not only suffer each other but learn to work together. Which is something else again and far more difficult than anything friend Bob the Moses seems to be thinking it is or by results (may I say) he has yet proved that it is.

Man's environment is at the threshold of a great change. Moribund for five hundred years, architecture—environment's sum and substance—is coming alive again with a more organic character. And this is coming notwithstanding academicism, modernist, or internationalism. Yes, or all isms added up together. Organic architecture has gone world-wide as a principle on which a democratic civilization may enjoy its own soul if ever it enjoys one at all. And yet we as people are far behind the other great peoples of this world owing to the density of our provinciality (our self-satisfaction). Our riches, good instincts, and first-rate creative sensitivity are bedeviled by mass routine-education. The power-lusting boy so strong in his muscles is finding vision with a voice but he is still diffident to utter as he is slow to understand Principle.

Soon, seeing from above the belt with the eye of a natural mind (yes, there is such a "seeing"—we call it genius) we will not pass out as the latest edition of the Holy Roman Empire nor go out in terms of commerce nor pass away as the shortest lived, smart commercial fabric in history, but, by way of a natural (or organic) architecture, we will become the greatest builders of all time for all time. What we need most though is to resolve to begin again with these principles of an organic architecture at the beginning, and learn to build more naturally for our own people with our own natural resources used for mankind. Our life is so different from anything antique! And yet *when* we build we could well build in a spirit not unlike that which inspired the noblest environments which man has ever made for himself in the past.

I stand here with you at noble old Princeton tonight because a profound natural is standing here with me, he who should have been standing here long before me to receive the blessing and good speed of Princeton prestige. You all know I mean "Leibermeister" Louis H. Sullivan: today little better understood than then. He would have kicked the presumptuous functionalist, with cart but no horse, off his doorstep as I did in his name some years ago. And yet perhaps it is characteristic of a social life like ours that any great cause must grow as much by meretricious imitators as by meritorious originators. So few men among us can take a principle straight. And, too, nearly every power-boy is a shopper. Dilution brings the whole matter more easily within his average range.

It is my hope that we the American people will grow in firm belief that no great environment is possible to the "also ran," be he a man or added up to his sum-total—a civilization. It is from within (from his own soul) that the man of our day will find inspiration to build anew, as he must, those buildings which are free because he is. What I am calling the Cart (the dogma—"form follows function") must have the horse (I am calling Inspiration the horse) *from within* before we can go anywhere in architecture, especially before we can move toward the great environment, those pure new structural forms of glass and steel for which Democracy searches either consciously or unconsciously. Eventually we will erect the great civic structure we desire. Unfailing faith in Vision will bring that enlightenment to the enormous lust of our young republic.

SECTION VIII

IMPRESSIONS
AND CONCLUSIONS

INTRODUCTION

BY THOMAS H. CREIGHTON

THE flow of subject matter through the Conference papers which have been presented is so obvious, and the positions stated so clear, that there will be no attempt here to recapitulate. The social and human basis of design was first established; various people expressed opinions on the limitations which encumber architecture's fulfillment and the possibilities which are open; the philosophical, psychological, even the physiological basis for form were discussed; the implications to architectural education of the foregoing were considered; more specific applications of the general bases were taken up in relation to extensive planning and the design of buildings.

What does this all add up to? Is it merely a lot of words? (One of my editorial associates thinks that this period in man's development, in distinction to the Stone Age and the Iron Age, should be known as the Verbi-age.) Or is there a useful purpose in discussing where we are going in architecture and why? Henry Churchill believes that developing a "philosophy and an esthetic of architecture and planning are . . . not barren exercises in words but a sorely needed clarification." And yet, along with all of the expressions of appreciation that were sent to the planners of the Conference by those who had attended—expressions that called the gathering "interesting," "instructive," "stimulating," "the most interesting meeting of architects I have ever attended," and so on—a few sour notes appeared. One participant felt that he had completely wasted his time. A prominent architect who was not at the Conference read news reports of it (*Time* spoke of "75 Architects Against the World") and wrote to friends at Princeton that it all sounded very foolish. It is interesting and perhaps significant that most of the men who saw nothing of value in the statements are fairly conservative in their design attitudes. It is possible that they may have felt a threat to established positions in the conceptions that emerge from the various papers. On the other hand, a group of advanced students from Princeton sat in on the meetings, and one of their number felt called upon to answer the protesting architect mentioned above. Politely he explained that reports in the press had been incomplete if not inaccurate, and he explained what he, as a student of architecture, had seriously received from the discussions. His name is William D. Wilson. He wrote, in part, as follows:

The most significant thing to me about the several sessions was the spontaneous recurrence at random of several themes. These themes insistently recurred in spite of a Conference program which attempted and largely succeeded in channeling the discussion quickly through the various aspects of planning man's physical environment. Obvious though some of these recurring themes may seem, I would attach a great deal of significance to them simply because they seemed to designate fields of general agreement upon which men of the architectural and allied professions might meet. Here is an incomplete list of these recurring themes:

1. Architectural education must reaffirm humanistic values. The proper study of architecture is man.

2. The machine must be humanized if its application to architectural techniques and esthetics is to be of valuable significance.

3. The architectural profession must make a greater effort to tell the public about the better physical environment within their reach if they want it.

4. The profession must take a more active role in bringing about the legislation which affects architectural planning.

5. The architect must be the coordinator of teams of specialists including not only designers and engineers but also city planners, sociologists, and political specialists as well.

In spite of the sporadic attempts of several delegates to introduce the issue of reaction vs. progress, I would not

classify this as one of the dominant notes of the Conference. Nor was the old story of traditional vs. modern.

Several things are interesting about the foregoing. In
the first place, the recurring theme, through several sessions, of what Professor Sherley W. Morgan called "the
reaffirmation of faith in the abiding humanistic values of
architecture" impressed Wilson, as a student observer, as
well as most of the participants. Several of the papers that
follow mention it as one of the important dominant themes.
One wonders how it could have been lost sight of for so
long that it becomes news. The other significant aspect of
Mr. Wilson's comment is that he, as a student, did not feel
an important divergence between "traditionalists" and
"modernists." Dean Bennett, in comments that follow, did
sense a division—not on those obvious grounds because, as
he says, all of the discussants might be considered in the
"more liberal" segment of the profession—but between
those who have "half-conscious reservations" and those who
"have wholly given themselves to the contemporary movement."

Whether such a division existed or not, it should be apparent to anyone who reads all of the statements that it was
not a point of controversy. This was not the usual battle
along those lines, but rather a serious attempt to define the
roots of architecture in our time. Most of the participants
felt that it was that very thing that Dean Bennett asks for—
an attempt to "lose ourselves as architects in the study of
architecture."

The reader will see in the several following papers that
each individual got something different from the discussion. Each one thought that certain things were most important, and no two agree as to what those things were—
except for the emphasis on humanism mentioned before.

Talbot Hamlin, Wells Bennett, and Henry Churchill
were sufficiently moved to contribute the evaluations that
follow. Within their statements, I believe, are contained
most of the reactions that followed the Conference. Except
for one. There lies in Princeton's archives an angry docu-

ment written on the way home by one participant who felt that the entire experience had been, not a waste of time, but frustrating and embarrassing. In cooler later moments he decided not to say for publication what he had written for the benefit of a few friends—and the archives—so the following quotation is anonymous. It is inserted here more to indicate that the gathering was capable of generating strong feelings than for its point of view, which is entirely that of one individual. It says in small part:

There were splendid parries and ripostes, brilliant use of quotations and of original and spontaneous epigrams. There were even a few moments of honest embarrassment when someone, say Catherine Bauer or Fred Adams or Carlos Contreras for a moment dared to break into the Gemütlichkeit to say something which stung for a second—these moments were too few. There were no agreements on principle, no agreements on action, no admission that we were living in a special time. . . .

It is possible to aver that the Conference was not a failure. Certainly at a similar Conference a decade ago there would have been many more (eclectics). . . .

Individualism reared its ugly head in many ways. . . . This theme of the individual nature of architecture and importance of the individual architect (to say nothing of his arrogance in assuming that, as coordinator, his talent must always make him as well the leader), this theme was so impelling throughout the Conference that it would be only painful to pile example upon example to prove the point.

There were a few moments of eloquence, to be sure; eloquence usually will stem only from sincerity and from the heart. . . . For my money the planners came off better than any other group—and from this statement I would not exclude even the cynical Robert Moses.

So "individualism rears its ugly head" even in reactions to and comments on the sum total of the symposium. The final conclusion-drawing in this book is left to Arthur Holden, Chairman of the Conference Committee.

TALBOT HAMLIN

INDUSTRIALIZATION: SERVANT OR MASTER?

BY TALBOT HAMLIN

Several valuable remarks by Talbot Hamlin have appeared in other sections of this book. He is introduced at the beginning of his paper in Section v on page 134.

AS I think of my memories of the exciting days in Princeton, one definite impression seems to dominate all others. Since it may have a certain significance, I somewhat hesitatingly state it here. This is the fact that underlying all the discussions and highlighting the most interesting controversies was a basic split in attitude, not only toward architecture but also toward the entire aims of modern living. This split was most clearly marked, it seems to me, and divided the speakers into two almost equal camps. It deals primarily with the attitude taken toward industry and industrial production.

One group thinks of industry as the servant of mankind, a means toward giving mankind more leisure and more power in order that he may cultivate a richer conscious existence and develop *all* sides of his nature to the highest degree. The other group seems to feel that industrial production and the products of industry are both such important factors that industrial thinking should control *all* of life, and that mankind in his wants and desires must limit himself to the things which our present notion of industry feels are logical industrial products, whether he likes them or not. The idea seems to be, "Here is what industry produces; you had better like it, and you had better stop wishing for anything else. It is good for you, because it comes from machines. Therefore, base your life on it, or else . . ."

The first attitude, the one we might call humanism, puts man's whole conscious and emotional life at the top; it was most brilliantly and poetically expressed in the eloquent paper read by Ernest J. Kump. The second attitude was brilliantly expressed in several statements made by Serge Chermayeff. George Howe seemed to hesitate between the two concepts. And it is particularly interesting that the most complete support of the humanist position came from an architect responsible for such revolutionary modern structures as the Acalenes High School and the Fresno City Hall.

This basic controversy is one of the most vital problems facing contemporary life. It has wide implications, sociologically and economically as well as politically. For the architect it means a new examination into the basic purposes of building and communities and the kind of life which in his design he hopes to produce or assist. This is a side of architectural thinking that has been too little emphasized. *Communitas*, by Percival and Paul Goodman, seems the only book I can think of which deals primarily with this engrossing subject. I feel that the fact that this question of basic attitude appeared so vitally as a controlling element in the Princeton Bicentennial Conference was one of the most valuable contributions which the Conference made.

ATTITUDES TOWARD ARCHITECTURE

BY WELLS I. BENNETT

Dean of the College of Architecture and Design at the University of Michigan, Wells Bennett has given much time and thought to the question of trends in architecture. In papers he has written, symposia conducted at the school of which he is the head, and in his capacity at times as an officer in the AIA, he has often indicated his concern as a critic and educator with the fact that our design today is "high as to space planning, so-so as to structural integrity, and low in qualities of beauty." From this position he analyzes in the paper that follows the discussions in previous sections.

IT SEEMS obvious that the architects taking part in this discussion are more liberal than the average of the architectural profession. The papers and related discussions, however, indicate considerable confusion among us. We are beyond doubt men of good will toward the planning of man's physical environment, but either we are proceeding from different premises or there persists a variance of reaction to premise that prevents our mutual understanding. What so troubles the waters? Surely we do not willfully resist a spirit of agreement.

Assuming that one can see the progressive group objectively, its members fall pretty readily into two categories. There is the considerable group of those who term themselves modernists but who have half-conscious reservations. These men sincerely and warmly endorse progress, but they cannot help feeling that in the last fifty years something of the glory has departed. Modern architecture seems to them tentative and impoverished. It rates their intellectual acceptance, but it has not won their hearts. In general, these are the older men.

On the other hand, those who have wholly given themselves to the contemporary movement have—likewise only half-consciously—come to assume that contemporary architecture is *fait accompli*, that since the reactionary rascals have been tossed out a new architecture has necessarily taken its place. They think they are in the groove. These men are mostly young. There remain a few pioneers of the new movement. They are not so complacent.

But whether we as individuals are slightly nostalgic or warmly content to be modern, the differences are only those of freshmen from different prep schools. We are not confused as to premises. It is a division that time will heal.

In exploring our attitudes further we may use a recognized check-list of architectural criticism:

Adequacy of space planning.
Structural integrity.
Esthetic quality.

To be sure, definitions of the constituent elements of a work of architecture are elusive in use, but we could no doubt amicably discuss their relative validity as evidenced in given examples. Should it be stated that the level of architecture being done today is high as to space planning, so-so as to structural integrity, and low in qualities of beauty, everyone would understand though we might not agree. Probably we should mainly prove that the factor of esthetic enhancement of man's environment is highly elusive. There would, however, be no confusion.

Basically our differences appear to arise from a conflict of personalities, from a trait of human nature at variance with the object of our Conference. Such strong expressions of personality are a by-product of individualism, and in Western civilization we are traditionally proud of this characteristic. Its release of energy and imagination provide excitement in life and lend great brilliance to our scene. How to preserve the values of individuality while merging our opinions in constructive tolerance is the essential problem. Frederic Towndrow's tart statement is to the point: "In looking back over the centuries and in noting how the great styles arose out of true building . . . the gravest doubts have arisen in my mind as to the virtues of the architect."* We could resolve our differences and reach ready understandings if we could lose ourselves as architects in the study of architecture. For instance, let the architect who designs a house yield something of the new, and to him, enhanced way of life into which his fascinated client is being fitted, to an objective study of *the* house and the institution of the family today. Whether the dwelling is obviously initialed by the designer is surely less important than that it be a good house. To do less than merge our effort is to prefer confusion to progress.

* *Architecture in the Balance*, by Frederic Edward Towndrow, Chatto and Windrus, London, 1933. p. 49.

SPACE, TIME, AND PEOPLE

BY HENRY S. CHURCHILL

Mr. Churchill, who was introduced to the reader on page 132, here returns the discussion to the opening theme—the relationship of man, natural environment, and manmade environment.

WHAT is most interesting to me in the discussions is that, in spite of their diffuseness, there are repeated over and over, in many ways and from many points of view, two themes. The first of these is the space-time complex, most ably presented in George Howe's paper. Here is the common denominator of today's architectural thinking: how to relate space to the new concepts of time and motion, to a new sense of man's place in the universe. The second theme is that of people, that planning and architecture must deal not merely with things but with the use people make of things, spiritually as well as materially; of the deep and primary relation which still exists—and which Arthur Morgan so well insists must be reinforced—between man and nature not as he splits it into atoms but as it exists for him tactually and visually and emotionally. Here again is a reflection of a wholly different attitude, a reflection of the growing consciousness that the more the material world disintegrates into particles, the more fluid our time and space becomes, the greater the need for psychological roots, for esthetic satisfactions, for a revaluation of man's relation to the Unknown. Man must in some way become one with his environment again, and since man is now creating more of this environment in his own image, the less he accepts it as Nature gives it, the greater the weight that rests on the architect and planner to comprehend and express what is the real meaning of his constructions.

A philosophy and an esthetic of architecture and planning are thus not barren exercise in words, but a sorely needed clarification. The significance of the papers and the flow of talk at Princeton therefore is in extracting the common denominator as a beginning of such a philosophy and such an esthetic. For we are at the start of a new age; we are groping for form, for an extension of our vision, for an integration of our art with a concept of a world held together not by material forces but by the force alone of man's all-pervading mind.

By themselves, the new technologies are nothing. It is what we do with them that will make us or break us as a biological species. What we do with them will depend on our concepts of our place in the universe, of our purpose in being in the universe at all. It is well, therefore, that we give attention, from time to time, to more than the surface of our paper, to directions other than those of the lines drawn by our pencils.

CONTACTS PRODUCE IDEAS

BY ARTHUR C. HOLDEN

THERE are few ideas that are wholly original. Originality is rather the form or conception that is added to a received impression when it is passed on to others by the recipient. Ideas are the product of human contacts. They quicken as the interchange of thought becomes more understanding and more stimulating.

Ideas vary in the stimulus which they produce. Ideas can be grasped only by those who are attuned to them. Much that was discussed by the Princeton Conference was of value principally to those with technical training. The purpose of the Conference was to furnish stimulus. The appeal was to those who may influence the direction of planning for man's physical environment in the future.

It is significant that professional men of contrasting viewpoints and specialized approaches could work open-mindedly together during the Conference. Diversities of emphasis were, of course, apparent. There was no effort made to reach conclusions but rather to illuminate advances that are under way along the entire frontier of human endeavor.

In the mind of the Chairman it was the intangibles that represented the real benefit of the Conference; it was the strengthening of convictions that something worth striving for remained to be mastered; it was the realization that others felt that new possibilities existed which, though as yet beyond our range, might ultimately be realized through seeking, through cooperation, and through understanding. Perhaps the Chairman, who had had the benefit of contact with the majority of the participants during a period of preparation extending over a full year, had hopes for the Conference which were too highly pitched. He was obliged to take his satisfaction like Browning's Rabbi Ben Ezra who said: "All I aspired to be and was not, comforts me!"

The Chairman was brought down to earth by the representative of the University, who wrote, saying that procedure required a succinct, itemized statement for publication, summarizing the achievements of the Conference. To this request, the Chairman replied that while the purpose of the Conference had been not so much to reach conclusions as to clarify the approach to planning man's environment, nevertheless there were very large areas of agreement which might be briefly summarized as follows:

1. It was pointed out that architects and engineers must possess highly specialized knowledge with regard to the uses of particular types of buildings. Designers must be skilled in analyzing the special problems of hospitals, health centers, libraries, schools, railroad stations, warehouses, theaters, residences, and other modern structures.

2. Social uses and social forms are constantly changing. Design must keep abreast of changing needs and learn to overcome the lags which retard progress.

3. Great progress is constantly being made in the production of new materials and in improved methods of construction. To make the best use of these advances, design must simplify its forms to conform to the new materials. It should provide for a greater degree of standardization and for the interchangeability of parts through modular measurements.

4. The attempt must be made to overcome the lags due to obsolete building regulations, and to certain habits of engineer-

ing and finance based upon conclusions that have been frequently dictated by specific experiences with the more limited materials of the past.

5. There must be a knowledge of man's psychological adaptability. There must be recognition of the importance of space, form, line, mass, color, the preservation of natural beauty, and a sense of orderliness with regard to purpose.

6. It must be recognized that esthetic values cannot be created through conscious aim, but are the evidence of an innate harmony that has been achieved through the arrangement of space in such a way that human needs and senses are satisfied.

7. One of the great problems of the day is the design and redesign of cities and communities. The design of cities calls for cooperation by highly trained specialists. Thorough understanding of the many factors involved is essential for the coordination of the design of cities.

8. We must recognize that our cities have outgrown human scale; we must restore vitality to local neighborhoods and readjust our social and political organization so as to approximate human scale.

9. The design of modern buildings also requires the process of analysis and coordination. Satisfactory results cannot be achieved by either eclecticism or imitation; a decent respect must be paid to the achievements of the past which represent a part of our cultural history.

10. It must be recognized that we suffer today from two kinds of mistakes made in the past. Some of our forebears, with their eyes on immediate needs only, erected shoddy ill-conceived structures which still plague us today. Others built too securely, forgetful that man of one generation was seldom capable of judging what was fit to be permanent through succeeding generations.

11. In the field of industrial design, we must recognize the significance of mechanization and apply the same standards of analysis and understanding to the design of individual objects as we have learned to apply to the design of modern buildings and as we are trying to develop in connection with redesign of cities and small communities.

In contrast to these areas of agreement, two differing emotional reactions were in evidence throughout the Conference. On the one hand, there was eagerness to make the most of new conceptions of design and to discard slavish adherence to habits and forms, produced by the living conditions of the past. On the other hand, there was fear lest new forms might sweep away the heritage of the past and cut off the average man from the sense of security which is derived from the acceptance and evidence of the substance left by the past.

But there are many types of men and they are differently affected by a sense of security. To many, security is little more than a sense of complacency engendered by an unreasoning belief that men can be happy gliding along from day to day following the course of least resistance. For such men, the guide posts of the past are essential to relieve them of the feeling that it is necessary to chart a course of their own. The majority of men, however, are, perhaps, almost completely anesthetic to their surroundings. It takes a violent shock or a new experience to wake the masses out of their lethargy.

On the other hand, there are men who have cultivated an appreciation of the values of life, who are conscious of the slow processes of civilization, and who derive a creative joy from the consciousness that they have the power to add to the values which they have inherited from the past. To such as these, the esthetic contemplation of the evidences of beauty produced by their fathers offers a sense of security, which lifts them up to aspiration and endeavor. It is the understanding, not the mere acceptance of the past that points the way to progress. The fear that contact with the experience of the past may be lost is very different from the terror that accompanies unreasoning resistance to change. It is understanding both of the spirit of the past and of the new needs that nurtures the spirit of progress.

There is no question but that the general spirit of the Conference was progressive. Within the limits of a two-day session it was hardly possible to discuss details, or to touch upon questions usually considered outside the field of design which have, nevertheless, exerted a limiting effect upon design. The relation of the problems of land and finance to planning man's physical environment were suggested as questions for discussion. Barring a reference to the fact that the control of land and of finance rested in hands other than the designer, the Conference agreed to side-step this issue. Impatience even was shown by some with the discussion of lags and habit which have limited the freer use of new materials and methods of construction. Nevertheless, it was recognized that the public must look to the designer for liberation from the restraints of obsolete building codes.

When it came to a question of economic restraints, the Conference seemed to turn its attention elsewhere. It was not brought out that the imaginative ingenuity of the designer, the architect, the planner might be applicable in the field of economics and public relations. The imaginative thinker, the creator of new ways is certainly needed to overcome the inertia of stereotyped methods of finance. It will be necessary to explore the motives of the decision to build in order to enlarge the limits within which decisions may be made as to how to build.

Subsequent to the Conference on Planning Man's Physical Environment, the Chairman was asked several times to speak on what took place at Princeton. He found himself saying that the outstanding contribution had been made by Ames of the Hanover Eye Institute. Ames's experiments have demonstrated that the truth, which we think we see, is not finite but is, in reality, an interpretation necessarily based upon accumulated experiential data. As men increase their understanding of past experiences, their capacity for perception is increased proportionately. The critical and analytical discussion of the Conference seemed to benefit all who took part and to strengthen the particular convictions and points of view of the participants.

Even though many architects were present, it was not the purpose of the Conference to give professional architects an opportunity to discuss their particular problems of design. Its purpose was to create an opportunity for thinkers, both inside and outside the field of professional design, to get together to discuss the sort of environment that is socially and psychologically desirable. It was intended to be an opportunity for architects to ask themselves how they had met the challenge of the new day. It was believed that the stimulus of such a discussion might act as a leaven to raise the capacity of architects for achievement.

It was self-evident that professional designers have been backward in developing a technique for the discussion of design problems. Certainly if the public is to achieve a better understanding of meaning and significance of good design, architects, engineers, and planners in general must have better and more frequent meeting grounds for the interchange of ideas. Until professional men have learned to make themselves understood by their fellows they can hardly be expected to make themselves understood by the public.